HEIKKINEN + KOMONEN

HEIKKINEN + KOMONEN

INTRODUCTION BY JUHANI PALLASMAA
EDITED BY WILLIAM MORGAN

THE MONACELLI PRESS

First published in the United States of America in 2000 by
The Monacelli Press, Inc.
10 East 92nd Street, New York, New York 10128.

Library of Congress Cataloging-in-Publication Data
Heikkinen + Komonen / introduction by Juhani Pallasmaa ;
edited by William Morgan.
p.   cm.—(Work in progress)
Includes bibliographical references.
ISBN 1-58093-020-4
1. Heikkinen-Komonen Architects. 2. Architecture, Modern—
20th century—Themes, motives. I. Morgan, William.
II. Series: Work in progress (New York, N.Y.)
NA1455.F53H455   1998
720'.92'2—dc21   98-29434

Printed in China

Designed by Pia Ilonen and Liisa Kause

Cover: Emergency Services College, Kuopio, Finland, 1992.
Photograph by Jussi Tiainen

Back cover: Villa Eila, Mali, Guinea, 1995.
Photograph by Onerva Utriainen

CONTENTS

Embassy of Nordic Countries, Berlin, Germany, Competition, 1994

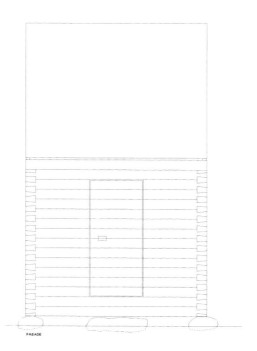

FASADE

Cottage for Architecture Park, Copenhagen, Denmark, 1996, and Stockholm, Sweden, 1998

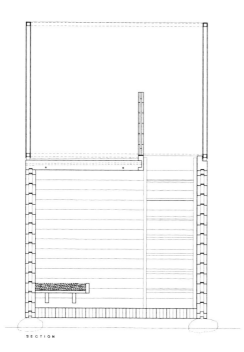

SECTION

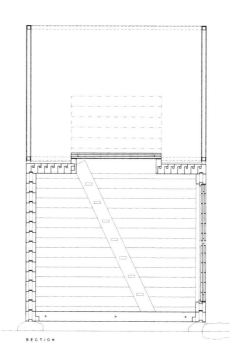

SECTION

ZEN AND THE ART OF MAKING ARCHITECTURE

CONCEPT AND DESIGN IN THE WORK OF HEIKKINEN - KOMONEN

Juhani Pallasmaa

At first glance, a building by Mikko Heikkinen and Markku Komonen could be taken merely as an example of the currently fashionable minimalist visual aesthetic. Their architecture, however, is firmly rooted in the traditions of Finnish and international modernism. It is an architecture of assimilation and amalgamation rather than exclusion, of essence rather than visual image. It draws equally on contemporary minimalist sculpture and humanity's archaic symbolic constructions, on pragmatic vernacular architecture and the mysteries of cosmic geometry and time.

The product of a process of condensation and distillation, the architecture of Heikkinen - Komonen fuses together programmatic, functional, and technical parameters with a dense projection of contextual references. For this team context is interpreted as humankind's conceptual situation in place and time rather than as constituting simple characteristics of the actual site. Beneath its reductive and laconic surface, the architecture aspires to an epic scope. Komonen cites a statement by Constantin Brancusi, "Simplicity is not a goal in art, but an end result," as the artistic credo of the partnership.[1] Authoritative simplicity in art is always a result of a process of compression rather than reduction. Komonen underlines the importance of artistic condensation in his citation of Anton Chekhov's instruction to Maxim Gorky: "Your only fault is your lack of restraint and lack of grace. When someone expends the least amount of motion on a given

action, that's grace. You tend to expend too much . . . Color and expressivity in nature descriptions are achieved through simplicity alone, through simple phrases like 'the sun set,' 'it grew dark,' 'it began to rain.' "[2] The collaborative duo of Mikko Heikkinen and Markku Komonen strives for elegance through a minimum number of moves. But these moves are calculated to engage the essentials.

The firm's architecture often reflects a high-tech ambience; however, its work seems to echo the technological poetry of the pioneering generation of modernists, such as Pierre Chareau and Jean Prouvé, more than today's virtuoso high-tech style. At the same time, the architects are critical of the machine aesthetic. "Elevating technology to a fetish, a Machine Romanticism, was an expression of puberty in architecture as well as in other areas of culture," writes Komonen.[3] The two clearly take an unromantic attitude toward technology in general. Their pragmatic outlook in regard to technology, structure, and material is reflected in the firm's recent projects in Guinea, West Africa, which utilize local construction methods, skills, and materials (for example, stabilized earth and unsawed wood and bamboo). The lyrical mood of these elemental projects reveals the power of an architectural idea to poetize construction regardless of the presence or lack of technical sophistication.

The architects aspire to a distinct quietness in order to clear the stage for the activities for which their

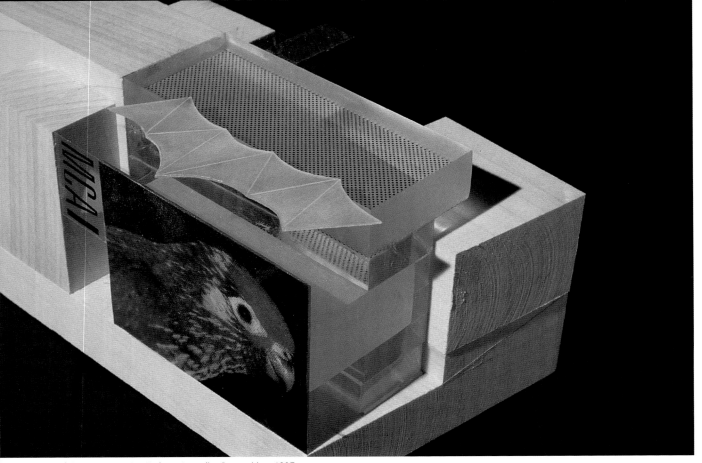

Museum of Contemporary Art, Sydney, Australia, Competition, 1997

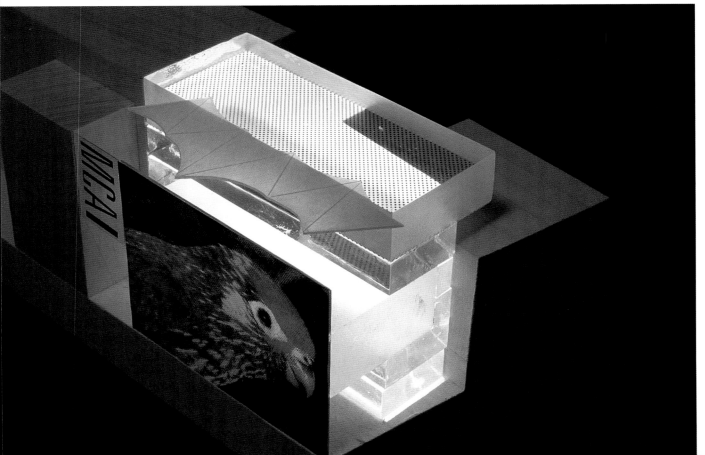

buildings are intended, whether it concerns establishing a sense of domesticity and home, creating an environment for work, or displaying objects of art to reveal their full emotive power. They remain cognizant, however, that a stylistically reductive minimal space is usually far from being neutral; a space that creates supportive neutrality has to have rich invisible undercurrents and reverberations. A vivid gray is composed of all colors.

The well-trained team of Mikko Heikkinen and Markku Komonen is the latest link in the chain of Finnish rationalism, which began with the proclamation of an "iron and brain style" by Sigurd Frosterus and Gustaf Strengell in 1904 in their influential pamphlet against the nationalistic romantic tendencies occurring at the turn of the century.[4] The rationalist credo was so convincingly argued that it brought the entire National Romantic movement to a sudden end. Their espousal of a sane architecture is once again valid in light of the current frantic search for publicity-grabbing and novelty.

In the subsequent history of Finnish architecture, a classical and rationalist tendency, based on a clear articulation of structure, has alternated with a romantic and expressionist orientation that emphasizes idiosyncratic shape and space. The first tendency is internationally oriented and articulates social concerns, whereas the latter approach elaborates regionalist themes and stresses a romantic concept of individuality. Constructivist rationalism, which developed after the late 1950s, dominated Finnish architectural thinking at the time Mikko Heikkinen and Markku Komonen both began their studies at the Helsinki University of Technology in 1968—the year of the Paris Spring, which had a powerful impact on the self-identity of Finnish architects. Traditionally apolitical Finnish architects, "trustees of the client" in accordance with the code of the Association of Finnish Architects, were suddenly drawn into the middle of a heated political debate on social injustice, misuse of resources, and global pollution. The essence of architecture as a form of art was questioned altogether. No doubt, this air of disillusionment strengthened the sense of reality of the duo, but eventually it also strength-

ened their convictions about the artistic nature of architecture.

The young Finnish constructivist generation of the 1960s was composed of former students of Aulis Blomstedt and Aarno Ruusuvuori; and the movement drew its inspiration from the structural classicism of Mies van der Rohe, Russian and Central European constructivism of the 1920s, the California rationalists of the late 1940s and early 1950s associated with *Arts & Architecture* magazine, and even from traditional Japanese architecture. Blomstedt, who had been educated in the 1920s in the pioneering spirit of functionalism, and Ruusuvuori, who had risen against the postwar romantic movement in Finland, had both left their teaching posts at the Faculty of Architecture of the Helsinki University of Technology by the time Heikkinen and Komonen arrived. But Blomstedt's ethical stance and appreciation of peasantlike restraint as well as Ruusuvuori's minimalism, which combines Brutalist concrete surfaces with elegantly ethereal detailing, remained enduring influences. Blomstedt was engaged in a fervent study of the harmonic principles of architecture. As a devoted Pythagorean, he represented a tradition that has persisted for more than two thousand years. In their writings, Heikkinen and Komonen echo Blomstedt's affection for naturalness and simplicity, and his preference for proportions based on small numbers as opposed to the more mystical proportional system of the golden section.[5]

During the 1960s Alvar Aalto was the overpowering figure of the Finnish architectural scene. The constructivist group, however, provided a programmatic counterpoint to the expressive and romantic approach of the aging academician. Although the work of Heikkinen - Komonen bears little similarity to Aalto's architecture, it has hardly managed to escape inspiration from the master.

In addition to the history of Finnish modernism, ingredients of international modernism can be felt in the partners' work: the abstracted whiteness of continental functionalism, the Italian constructivist classicism of Giuseppe Terragni and Adalberto Libera, and the more recent structuralist strategies

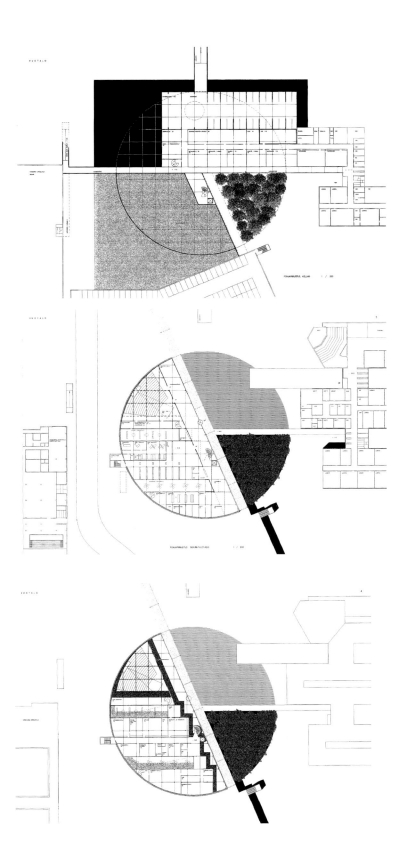

Vuotalo Cultural Center,
Helsinki, Finland, 2000

of Aldo van Eyck and Herman Hertzberger. The impassioned and forceful projects of Russian constructivism are evoked in their designs as well. The ideal of weightless flotation and movement brings to mind El Lissitzky and Kasimir Malevich, whereas the counterpoint of rectangles, circles, and arcs recalls the mythical projects of Ivan Leonidov.

The signature vocabulary of the team evolved through their competition projects and exhibition designs, and in their early executed work. They first achieved both professional maturity and public recognition in 1986 with their winning competition entry for the Heureka Finnish Science Center, in Vantaa. The architects' design strategy utilized elemental volumes, interpenetrating and intersecting one another in subtle skew displacements, with occasional curved elements. Three compositional strategies can be identified in the development of Heikkinen - Komonen's work: this collage of elementary rectangular, cylindrical, and arclike volumes and shapes; a dominant rectangular volume or linear bar with skewed volumetric and furnishing elements within the main volume or jutting out of it; and a static minimalist volume relying for its architectural impact on a sense of gravity, material, texture, transparency, color, and detail deriving from the logic of assembly.

The first strategy derives from constructivist and suprematist precedents; the second parallels deconstructivist tendencies; the third strategy resembles that of American minimalist sculpture. Heikkinen - Komonen's designs first progressed to greater complexity, from a planar juxtaposition of elements in the floor plan to seemingly arbitrary spatial configurations, in their competition project for the House of Culture in Nuuk, Greenland, and the playful Children's Cabin for a Housing Fair in Lahti. At present the firm seems to be moving toward a more static and mute expression, as exemplified by the tight rectangular packing of spaces in the competition projects for the Museum of Contemporary Art in Helsinki and the Waterfront Concert Hall in Copenhagen; the project for the Audiovisual Center for the University of Art and Design currently under construction in Helsinki; or the Max Planck Institute for Molecular Biology and Genetics in Dresden, now in its initial design phase. An asymmetrical suspension structure or a stretched canvas sail is frequently used as a playful counterpoint to the austere volume. The spirited project for a tiny unit in an allotment garden in Copenhagen, which contains a black-log cubicle on the ground level and an airy canvas frame of the same dimensions on top of it, open to the sky, exemplifies this tendency toward poetic reduction.

The exterior is often deceptive; the unassumingly simple selection of elements becomes a complicated spatial and formal game that at times achieves a Piranesian density, as in the spaces of the Finnish Embassy in Washington, D.C. The overlay of the structural grid, the secondary elements, and the quality of transparency create an unexpected experiential complexity. The visual image of a village frequently emerges, as in the two schemes for the Centers for Karelian Culture in Kuhmo, Finland, and Kostamus, Russia; the southern facade of the European Film College in Ebeltoft, Denmark; or the lobby of the Foibe Senior Citizen Housing and Amenity Center in Vantaa. Order plays against accident and arbitrariness, rigor against casualness, stasis against movement, opacity against transparency, lightness against gravity, form against image.

Modern architecture developed in a fertile cross-pollination with modern art. In the 1930s, however, architecture began to distance itself from the arts, and eventually confined itself to the constricting ideology of the International Style. During the past two decades, architecture has again sought inspiration from the arts. At the same time, sculpture has effectively stepped into the vacuum left by architecture; numerous contemporary sculptors have been actively engaged in the remythicizing and repoeticizing of site, for the purpose of turning an anonymous location into a specific place. Architects have again looked to the ways in which other art forms define humankind's existential ground. The current blurring of the borders between art and architecture has, however, caused as much confusion as authentic artistic liberation. Architects and educators have too often forgotten that architecture is a discipline fundamentally different from sculpture or other forms of art because of its essential engage-

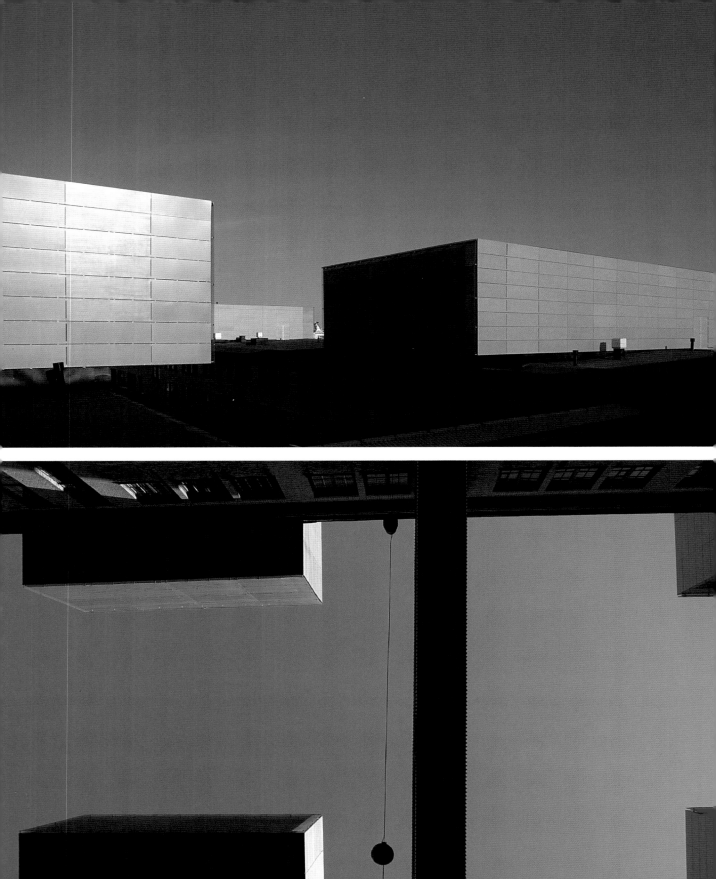

ment with the requirements of utilitarian space as well as the tectonic reality of construction.

The architectural approach of Heikkinen and Komonen is closely intertwined with the philosophy and aesthetics of minimalist and conceptual art. It is revealing that Markku Komonen celebrated his fiftieth birthday in 1995 by making a pilgrimage to Tîrgu-Jiu in Romania to see Constantin Brancusi's mythic environmental sculpture ensemble *Endless Column* (1938). Of the environmental piece, which creates an axis 1,493 meters long, he writes: "The endless play of proportions, based on the classical Greek study of harmony and religious symbolic numbers, is one of the rhizomes from which the magnetic quality of the work grows."[6]

For his part, Mikko Heikkinen made a trip to the American Southwest in 1992 to study Donald Judd's minimalist sculptural constructions at Marfa, Texas. "From different directions a volume is simultaneously solid and open," he notes of Judd's one hundred identical aluminum boxes. "The surface of a piece of sculpture may be seen as fully matte, or it may mirror the grass plains spreading around. One feels as if one is looking at a magician's mirror box; it is impossible to know whether a volume is open in reality, or whether one is looking at an illusion created by the mirroring surface. Light makes the edges of the volume appear cuttingly sharp, or makes them disappear and destroys the actual shape of the space."[7] He also points out that Judd based his work on the relations of small numbers, 1:2, 2:3, 3:4—another Pythagorean.

Heikkinen and Komonen have been inspired additionally by the work of Carl André, Robert Irwin, Walter de Maria, Agnes Martin, Gordon Matta-Clark, Robert Morris, Robert Smithson, and James Turrell, but they transfer these artists' minimalist imagery and aesthetic sensibility to the scale and tectonic reality of architecture. An architect must articulate the transition of scales from the distant image to the intimacy of the touching hand. A mere image in architecture is doomed to remain only a retinal picture unless it succeeds in convincing the viewer of his or her existence in the actual space of everyday realities. The art of architecture is to use momentary illusion for the ultimate purpose of reinforcing the experience of reality.

Both partners are equally interested in primordial human constructions and in contemporary earth art. In his inaugural lecture at the Helsinki University of Technology in 1995, Komonen elaborated on the archaic essence of the Greek word denoting the architectural profession, *Arkhitekton*, and the significance of the Minoan legend of the labyrinth and its maker, Daedalus, the world's first architect.[8] Heikkinen has written about the dolmens at Carnac, in France, as well as the mysterious earth architecture of Mound City in Chillicothe, Ohio, dating back more than one thousand years.[9] In the late 1940s Mound City so impressed Barnett Newman that he regarded "Egyptian pyramids as mere ornament."[10]

In comparison, Heikkinen has written enthusiastically about Richard Serra's environmental work *Afangar*, a configuration of eighteen paired basalt pillars on the treeless island of Videy, Iceland.[11] The firm's projects frequently include aspects of earth art, such as the geological map of Finland that adjoins the Finnish Science Center, the zones of vegetation that cut across the immense parking lot of the Arlanda Airport in Stockholm, or the rows of tubular perforated steel columns lining the automobile approach to the new Vuosaari residential district of Helsinki. The columns, lit from within, evoke the bonfires set in Vuosaari during World War II to divert enemy bombers from the city center.

In many of their projects Heikkinen and Komonen have incorporated architectural artworks that engage cosmic geometries and dimensions. These are frequently accomplished in collaboration with the Finnish conceptual and earth artist Lauri Anttila. The Finnish Science Center includes a wall with a polarizing metal surface that refracts light into a spectrum. The wall is juxtaposed with a steel-and-glass facade painted in the colors of the spectrum: an actual physical phenomenon is juxtaposed with its artistic presentation. A virtual enclosing

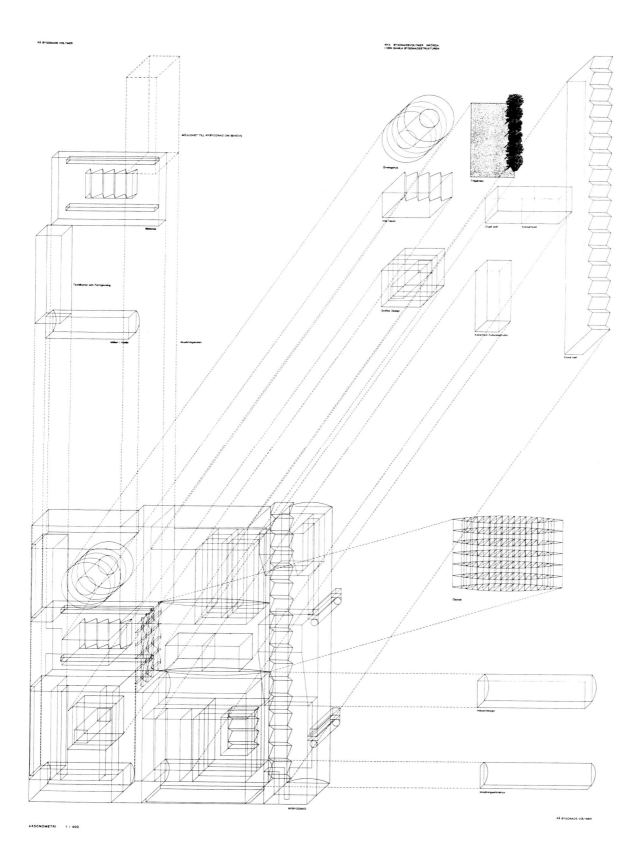

Artcampus, Four Art Academies, Stockholm, Sweden, Competition, 1995

frame consisting of the light of a rectangularly mirrored laser beam was to complete the work; regrettably, only the painted spectrum was executed.

In the Rovaniemi Airport a diagonal forty-meter-long skylight marks a precise location of the meridian of the Arctic Circle, which slowly moves between two extreme positions and last passed through the passenger lobby in 1990. A lens on the roof of the building reflects the rays of the midday sun on an analemma in the shape of an elongated figure eight, which is the projection of the elliptical orbit of the Earth. The curved white surface suspended from the lobby ceiling was conceived as a projection screen for scientific images of the northern lights. Because of a lack of understanding on the part of the client, the northern lights have never been projected on the screen, and this lobby space with cosmic messages has been vandalized by tasteless Santa Claus decorations installed by airport management.

The work of the team occasionally bears resemblance to conceptual art. The project Matrix H_2O Madrid is a conceptual scheme as much as a piece of environmental art. The minimal grid composition of linear patterns, hedges, and water pillars indicates the invisible underground reservoir system of the city. In the Finnish Embassy in Washington, the virtual horizontal plane that continues the floor plane as well as the structural grid outside across a wooded ravine also exhibits a conceptual character.

Beauty as a conscious aim in art tends to lead to sentimentality and kitsch. The most striking experience of beauty seems to be as a consequence of other concerns, such as an aspiration to clarity, precision, and order. In his book *Watermark*, the Russian writer Joseph Brodsky criticizes Ezra Pound for his too direct attachment to beauty: "*The Cantos*, too, left me cold; the main error was an old one: questing after beauty. For someone with such a long record of residence in Italy, it was odd that he hadn't realized that beauty can't be targeted, that it is always a by-product of other, often very ordinary pursuits."[12]

The two architects are suspicious of aestheticization. Mikko Heikkinen admires Walter de Maria's *The 2000 Sculpture* (1992) in the Kunsthaus Zurich, which is composed of 800 five-sided, 800 seven-sided, and 400 nine-sided gypsum bars set in parallel rows: "The layout seems to lack any artistic expression and personal commitment, seemingly one of those geometric matrices inspiring us to no more than a stifled yawn. Anything but that happens. The number of variables is limited, the composition of the elements is conscious and carefully implemented to the last millimeter. But one is not disturbed by having someone—the artist—dictating one's sensations. Paradoxically, the rigorous approach leaves the end open; the associations may run free like contemplating the sparkle of the sea or the leaves shivering in the breeze."[13]

Heikkinen expresses a clear sympathy for Donald Judd's approach to making art without any explicit message when he quotes Judd's statement "I don't know what has happened to the pragmatic, empirical attitude of paying attention to what is here and now; it's basic to science. It should be basic to art too. Only what can be known and experienced, is plausible. The truth emerges through concrete experiences, not through metaphysical constructions."[14]

Despite their affinity for visual art, Heikkinen and Komonen base their work on the rigorous criteria of rational logic and functional and technical performance, and on lessons learned from personal experience as well as the tacit wisdom of their craft. Regardless of the layering of thought, their designs represent an attitude of realism and reason. The architectural solution is frequently grounded in surprisingly straightforward and transparent ideas. The plan for the Air Patrol Squadron Base for the Finnish Frontier Guard in Rovaniemi derives from the "closest packing" of two Bell 412 helicopters, a Bell AB 206 and a Super Puma helicopter, and a light Piper Cherokee aircraft. The Emergency Services College in Kuopio, organized along a straight two-hundred-meter-long corridor, expresses the "confidence, promptness, prudence, and resolution"[15] required of rescue workers working with catastrophic circumstances such as fires and accidents.

Heikkinen and Komonen often take the pragmatic aspects of the program and the limitations of the site as starting points to generate solutions. The overpowering wind conditions in Greenland generated an "empirical" architectural scheme for the Nuuk House of Culture. The competition project takes the direction of the prevailing wind and the visual image of immense blocks of ice, floating in an apparently chaotic configuration, as the starting point for the development of an architectural solution. Komonen's design for a birdhouse for an exhibition was made out of a board from the demolished concrete molds of their site for the Foibe Senior Center in Vantaa, a used cardboard tube for transporting drawings, and the remains of a wooden pencil. The linear zones of cracked rock that intersected the site of the Arlanda Air-Traffic Control Center competition project, unfit for construction, were pragmatically turned into a landscaping pattern. The inevitable becomes a design motif.

The team explores the tension between order and disorder, preconception and spontaneity. Its architecture is at once serious and playful, controlled and whimsical. To underline the importance of this balancing act, Komonen has often quoted Paul Valéry's maxim "Two things do not cease threatening the world, disorder and order."

While seeking architectural rigor, both Heikkinen and Komonen are attracted to commonplace occurrences of life. Heikkinen praises the bare interiors of Donald Judd's Chinati Foundation at Marfa: "All the layers of surfaces, furnishings, and decorations of a former banking hall were torn off. The old paint surfaces, eroded plaster, and paintings of a 1920s folk artist, revealed beneath, were left as they were found. The atmosphere is as in a Tuscan loggia. How often one would want to stop architecture in its phase of construction before gypsum plates and latex paints are added."[16] Komonen describes the magic of an image of an open window of his flat reflected on the opposite wall.[17] He also portrays the interior of a paper mill in northern Portugal as an unintentional example of monumentality in architecture: "In this dark space of production, warm paper pulp steamed. The figures of workers moved between the wedges of light sprouting from the small windows. The upper floor was made of wooden slats, through which light and fresh wind flooded. Across the space, cobwebs of metal wires were spanned, on which the completed sheets of paper were hung to dry. The smell of drying paper filled the silent space bathed in light. Muffled sounds of labor echoed from the lower floor."[18]

Mikko Heikkinen writes about the architectural experiences of his visit to a steel mill with equal fascination: "Emotionally speaking, perhaps the deepest effect on me has been made by architecture 'before the Fall,' that is, architecture that lacks a conscious aesthetic intention. What we saw really had us quaking. The hall completely lacked an aesthetic content or affectation. The endless rows of furnaces and rollers, cascades of molten steel and gigantic bales of steel sheets in the soot-blackened mill, represented a type of architecture and art that is never seen in exhibition halls. Natural architectural spaces—human-made or formed by nature—often have the same profound effect. When one drives through the regular planted rows of an olive grove one undergoes an unbelievable kinetic experience. A ravine formed by nature itself, a stone cathedral, has a greater effect than most human-made monuments."[19]

The architectural concepts of Mikko Heikkinen and Markku Komonen have created a signature style, unmistakably theirs, that nevertheless strives for an elimination of the individual designer through the inevitable universality and anonymity of reason and disciplinary skill. "The dissolution of the author's own signature into the whole, the definite secondariness of expression and medium, makes one think of the ancient Chinese legend of the Master of Archery who no longer needed bow nor arrows and who finally did not even remember the name of his instrument," writes Mikko Heikkinen.[20] This metaphor points at the Zen of architecture. "The greatest liberty is born of the greatest rigor," Valéry once said,[21] a credo to which Heikkinen and Komonen subscribe.

N O T E S

1. Markku Komonen, "Brancusin pöytä, portti ja päät-tymätön pylväs" (Brancusi's Table, Gate and Endless Column), *Helsingin Sanomat*, December 1, 1995, B3.

2. Markku Komonen, "Rakentamisen tekniikka ja taide" (The Technology and Art of Construction), *Arkkitehti*, April 1995, 93; Anton Chekhov, letter to Aleksey Peshkov (Maxim Gorky), January 3, 1899, in *Letters of Anton Chekhov*, ed. Simon Karlinsky, trans. Michael Heim and Simon Karlinsky (New York: Harper & Row, 1973), 338.

3. Komonen, "Rakentamisen tekniikka ja taide," 92.

4. "We have plenty of decorative and artistic talent here in Finland at present. What we need is some guiding, clear and rational force. It's men we need, men who are prepared to break irrevocably with the past, to look boldly and resolutely to the future. Men who are not merely heart and soul but are made more of brains and good sense, heroes of thought, more than those *Deren ganze Seele in den Augen steckt* [whose entire soul is in their eyes] . . . We want an iron and brain style." Gustaf Strengell and Sigurd Frosterus, *Arkitektur: en stidskift våra motståndare tillägnad of Gustaf Strengell och Sigurd Frosterus* (Architecture: A Challenge to Our Opponents by Gustaf Strengell and Sigurd Frosterus) (Helsinki: Euterpes Förlag, 1904; printed in English in *Abacus Yearbook* 3, Helsinki: Museum of Finnish Architecture, 1983), 49–79.

5. For a discussion of Blomstedt's theories, see *Aulis Blomstedt, Architect: Pensée et forme-études harmoniques*, ed. Juhani Pallasmaa (Helsinki: Museum of Finnish Architecture, 1977).

6. Komonen, "Brancusin pöytä, portti ja päättymätön pylväs."

7. Mikko Heikkinen, "Korkean taivaan alla—Donald Juddin arkkitehtuurista" (Under the High Skies—On Donald Judd's Architecture), *Arkkitehti*, January 1993, 62.

8. Komonen, "Rakentamisen tekniikka ja taide," 93.

9. Mikko Heikkinen, "Tila, aika ja arkkitehtuuri" (Space, Time and Architecture), *Arkkitehti*, January 1995, 74–76.

10. "Ohio, 1949," *Barnett Newman: Selected Writings and Interviews* (Berkeley and Los Angeles: University of California Press, 1992), 174.

11. Heikkinen, "Tila, aika ja arkkitehtuuri."

12. Joseph Brodsky, *Watermark* (London: Penguin Books, 1997), 70.

13. Mikko Heikkinen, "Dolmens and Disneylands," unpublished lecture presented at symposium on per-manence, Virginia Polytechnic, March 23, 1996.

14. Heikkinen, "Korkean taivaan alla," 63–64. "Interview of Donald Judd" (exhibition catalog, Kunstverein St. Gallen, 1990), 56.

15. *Heikkinen & Komonen* (Barcelona: Gustavo Gili, 1994), 30.

16. Heikkinen, "Korkean taivaan alla," 64.

17. Markku Komonen, unpublished photograph and note, July 7, 1994.

18. Komonen, "Rakentamisen tekniikka ja taide," 93.

19. *An Architectural Present—7 Approaches*, ed. Marja-Riitta Norri and Maija Kärkkäinen (Helsinki: Museum of Finnish Architecture, 1990), 179.

20. Mikko Heikkinen, "Ruumi maasmine" (The Return of Space), *Arkkitehti*, May-June 1994, 14.

21. Paul Valéry, *Dialogues*, trans. William McCausland Stewart (New York: Pantheon Books, 1956), 131.

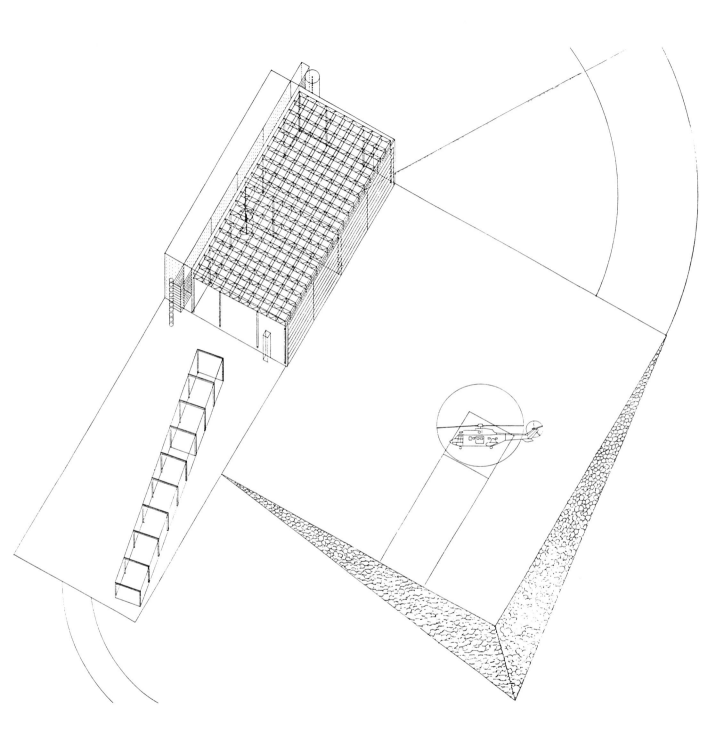

Air Base for the Finnish Frontier Guard, Rovaniemi, Finland, 1992

ONE TIGHT SNOWBALL

William Morgan

Images of the Winter War were on my mind when I flew to Lapland during a blizzard a few years ago. Long before I studied Finnish architecture, my strongest image of Finland had been one of soldiers skiing through the forest to hurl Molotov cocktails at invading Russian tanks. The sky, the woods below, and the runway were a mass of undifferentiated white. A battleship-gray building loomed out of the storm. Giant white letters, splashed billboard-fashion across it, spelled out ROVANIEMI, announcing Arctic Finland's new airport. This unexpectedly contemporary gateway to the northern reaches of the country was designed by architects Mikko Heikkinen and Markku Komonen.

The airport literally straddles the Arctic meridian. In contrast to the new wooden buildings of the Arctic Circle Visitors Center (where Santa Claus greets half a million tourists annually), the airport's tribute to geography is more universal, more cosmic. A long skylight parallels the polar latitude (nevertheless, the circular projection screen in the terminal and the sweeping entrance canopy are not postmodern signals of a polar circle motif). Closer to the mark is a grouping of granite steles—a sort of "Laphenge"—near the entrance marquee. There is an ineffably primitive aura about the airport, reflecting the nature of a country people who have only relatively recently moved to cities and become bankers, doctors, and designers. Even so, it is the elemental geometry of the thirty-three-by-fifty-four-meter steel box that gives the terminal its ironic timelessness.

Rovaniemi Airport challenges perceptions about Finnish architecture, which for most people *is* Alvar Aalto. He so dominated the architectural landscape of Finland that we know few names of other designers in this aesthetically literate land. His work is the object of pilgrimages to Finland, where "Alvaristi" expect northern reflections of the Bauhaus at Paimio Sanatorium, Le Corbusier's Villa Savoye-in-the-Woods at Villa Mairea, or the cozy brick of Wright Resurrected in the civic center at Säynätsalo. Aalto was the prophet from the edge of the world who gave modernism a human face.

Reima and Raili Pietilä explored a similar but more expressionistic path leading away from the International Style, although they are little known outside of Scandinavia. The Pietiläs created daring and enigmatic compositions, such as the public library in Tampere (inspired by such divergent totems as a mating grouse and Celtic manuscripts), while the cavelike residence of the President of Finland at Mäntyniemi speaks of the nation's mist-shrouded, pre-Christian past. And there is at Rovaniemi Airport a strong puff of what Reima Pietilä called Finnish architecture's "pagan incense." The new terminal says: the style is modern; the place is prehistory.

Not large (there are only four gates), the terminal is a metal box with wire-mesh ceilings suspended from concrete columns and exposed mechanicals. Yet the minimalist industrial aesthetic offers a deeply respectful homage to the world of reindeer

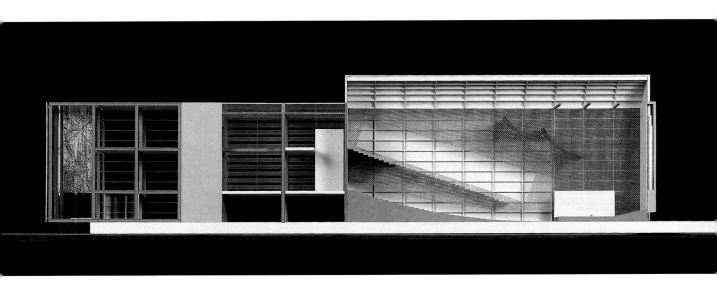

Waterfront Concert Hall, Copenhagen, Denmark, Competition, 1993

and lichen: something so obviously *human-made* as the airport acknowledges that we are but temporary builders on earth.

At the top of the world, is Rovaniemi more off the beaten path than Ronchamp or Bilbao? Isolated perhaps, but not silent, Rovaniemi rekindles the drama, excitement, and fear of flying. Unlike most spirit-deadening passenger-processing airports, Rovaniemi's suspension cables and exposed skeleton bring to mind the wiry sinews of World War I fighter planes, as well as a sense of the constructivist honesty of early modernism.

The beautifully proportioned cube set upon the snow serves as a reminder of functionalism's strength in Finland. The Mies-Aalto debate was not as one-sided as an outsider might believe, for a pure modernism has endured. Markku Komonen and Mikko Heikkinen were trained by disciples of Aulis Blomstedt, Aalto's pedagogical rival and influential preacher of rationalism. (Blomstedt once chided Aalto for what he saw as the declining quality of his former schoolmate's design, noting that during childhood snowball fights Aalto could make "one tight snowball.")

Heikkinen and Komonen's belief that architecture is not about style but about poetry achieved through program is evident in the Emergency Services College in Kuopio. Every Finnish fireman, paramedic, and ambulance driver is trained here, and the very program of teaching people to act calmly in the face of fire and mayhem is reflected in the complex's cool geometry of long narrow classroom block contrasted with crescent-shaped dormitory.

Kuopio also offers clues to some of the architects its designers admire—Tadao Ando, Louis Kahn, Luis Barragán, Le Corbusier—and it gives abundant cues to Heikkinen - Komonen's subsequent work. Besides the controlled, refined use of concrete, there is the ever-present formalism of circle and rectangle, as well as the signature screening—in this case, chain-link fencing stretched across the dormitory's curved facade.

Kuopio and Rovaniemi are hardly on the beaten path to anywhere, but Markku Komonen and Mikko Heikkinen's Finnish Embassy is in the heart of Washington, D.C. With its trellised facade of patinated bronze, the embassy is a revolutionary but well-mannered guest in stuffy and architecturally timid Washington. The green granite box gracefully responds to its small, steeply wooded site and disappears into the trees.

The exterior is as incredibly modest as the interior is dramatic—like the shy, reserved Finns who politely mask their passions. The sweeping maple-and-steel staircase beneath copper-clad cube-rooms suspended from the floor above, and the glass walls that dissolve the barrier between people inside and nature outside, are the kind of breathtaking gestures that astound the visitor. The pattern of lights—set flush in the entrance court, sparkling inside on the ceiling, and continuing outside, mounted on poles in the woods—becomes a metaphorical trail of Arctic stars.

Some critics contend that the embassy represents an "architecture of silence," but Komonen and Heikkinen simply have the wisdom of knowing when not to say something in order to make a point—through mystical denial substance is nourished. Here, the elemental box becomes a reliquary of spiritual memory. The embassy is one of Washington's contemplative spaces—like the Vietnam Memorial or the garden at Dumbarton Oaks. The sensitive, timeless spirit of the building, however, is found less in the ambience of Washington than in the American work of art the architects admire most, the Indian burial mounds of southern Ohio.

Rigorous geometry—as well as site specificity—underlies all of Heikkinen and Komonen's work. The repeated use of boxes and circles, along with metal screening and industrial materials, is not formula but total dedication to an ideal of pure form. The circle and the cube are the blank page upon which to inscribe an epic or a haiku. The universal container is to Heikkinen and Komonen what wood

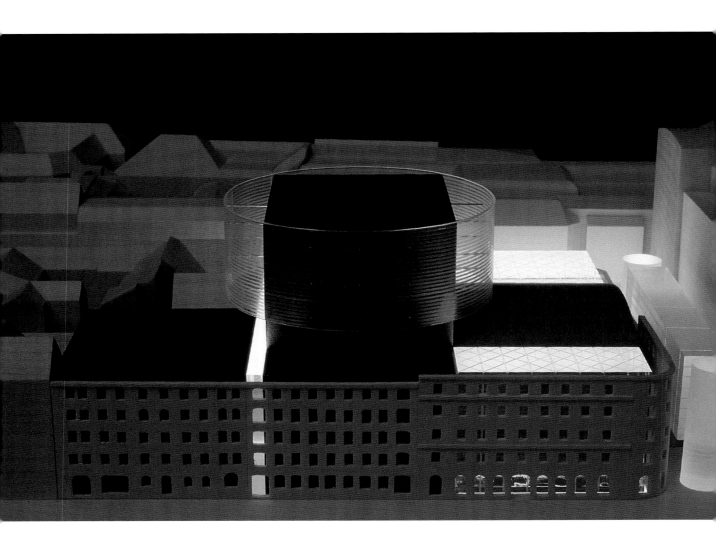

Royal Theater—New Theater, Copenhagen, Denmark, Competition, 1995

is to the Japanese temple builder or stone to the Mayan mason.

The architects' achievement lies in combining the high-tech world of corporate offices or a filling station with the minimalist spirit of a Mark Rothko canvas or a Donald Judd sculpture. The partners' work also recalls Edward Hopper and Charles Sheeler's elevation of grain silos and factories, barns and humble houses, to classic icons.

The Teboil Rajahovi Service Station in Vaalimaa is a large American-style truck stop at the main border crossing on the road to Saint Petersburg. Teboil's design marks a return to the initial concept of the filling station as a utilitarian structure. The face of the building is essentially the bold signage that advertises fuel prices and facilities, acknowledging that gas-station signs are often more important than the buildings behind them.

The truck stop's giant drum form is both oil tank and classical temple. The large circle of deep blue enamel visually outweighs all the commercial functions it has to carry (a sauna for truckers, a cafeteria, a grocery store, and other shops). Recalling the airport in Rovaniemi, the interior has an appropriately mechanical quality; the gray color scheme balances the visual chaos of this lively oasis/marketplace. Like the polar circle, Teboil marks a line, in this case Westernized Europe's frontier with Russia.

The Finnish headquarters of McDonald's, that ubiquitous purveyor of fast food and American culture, provides another opportunity for the architects to restate their theory of functionalism. Rather than design overtly pop roadside architecture (or play on the fact that the Golden Arches were inspired by Finnish-American architect Eero Saarinen's design for the Saint Louis Arch), Heikkinen and Komonen relied on the stability of the circle, combining contemporary materials with ancient but still relevant forms. Layered in bands of alternating glass and dark green alu-

minum panels, McDonald's is understatedly handsome—more Adolf Loos than suburban strip. The world's best-known logo is subtly ghostwritten in the spruce trellis-as-screen that wraps this six-story office block.

Although the heart of an important business enterprise, the corporate offices are almost monastically spare, while the restaurant itself is among the most elegant in the entire chain. The Finnish architects make informed references to the 1950s, the decade McDonald's first appeared. A ceiling sculpture—butterfly chairs strung together centipede-fashion—hangs above a mural depicting a 1954 McDonald's; the original store's canopy is replicated in neon.

At first glance, the McDonald's Headquarters might appear to be another manifestation of European fascination with glitzy 1950s American culture. In the hands of these Finnish designers, however, commercial icons are transformed into ironic, contemplative touchstones—like the trail of stars in Washington or the Arctic Circle at Rovaniemi. Without parody—and without recourse to the obvious vocabulary of Robert Venturi, Charles Moore, or Claes Oldenburg—the architects respectfully acknowledge the influence of America. McDonald's is as much about memory as is the Finnish Embassy.

Perhaps being linked with such a high-profile name as McDonald's will bring Heikkinen - Komonen the well-deserved recognition that has thus far eluded the firm. But celebrity should not be confused with art; as tough and as unyielding as the Samurai warrior whose manual inspired the program for the rescue school at Kuopio, Komonen and Heikkinen are not about to compromise their beliefs to secure commissions.

The architecture of Mikko Heikkinen and Markku Komonen is like the young Alvar Aalto's perfect, hard-packed snowball: it lacks superfluous ornament and has no more or no less than what it needs to score a direct hit.

McDONALD'S HEADQUARTERS

Helsinki, Finland, 1997

Urban structure of central Helsinki with McDonald's Headquarters on the western border

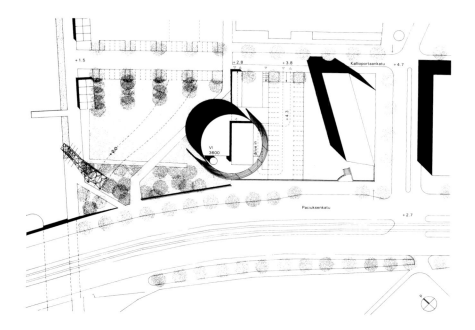

The cylindrical McDonald's Headquarters building resembles a corner tower in an imaginary town wall, this one on the southwestern edge of an urban development. The unobstructed site makes the facade publicly accessible and visible from all directions, whether it is approached from the Helsinki city center or from the west, as well as from the north, from the area of Pikku Huopalahti, effectively creating an "end" for its picturesque city-planning project of the 1980s.

The McDonald's Headquarters includes a hamburger restaurant, a small training center, and offices. The supporting structure and the interior of the building are set within Cartesian coordinates, around which is wrapped a continuous window that provides a panorama of the landscape. There is a view to the outside from every location in the building, and each level is open and transparent. The landscape and the site are constantly present in the interior. The sunny side has a

wooden trellis on a steel structure; the wood is glue-laminated, heat-treated spruce, known as Thermowood. This treatment method, developed by the State Technical Research Center, increases the weather-resistance of soft woods to the level of tropical species without the use of impregnating agents. The facade is of greenish glass and powder-painted matte-finish aluminum sheet, which is fastened with open joints to corrugated steel weatherproofing. Instead of the more usual lightweight aggregate, the flat roof is covered with crushed recycled glass.

For the restaurant, the client wanted to re-create some of the atmosphere of the 1950s and the first standardized McDonald's restaurants, designed by the American architect Stanley Meston. The painting on the restaurant wall by Pekka Mannermaa celebrates the classic McDonald's built in 1954 in Des Plaines, Illinois. Transparent glass walls permit patrons to see

through to the kitchen, as was customary in the 1950s, and be assured that high-level hygiene is observed in food preparation. A sculpture by Kari Cavén called *The Flight of a Bat* hangs from the ceiling; its form was derived from the design of the classic 1950s butterfly chair—or bat chair, as it is called in Finnish.

The client did not require that the design be readily identifiable as a McDonald's building, nor did it demand compliance with the company's design manuals. The incorporation of the logo as part of the architecture and town-scape originated from the sign's own graphic and sculptural potential. Attached to a sound-proof wall coated with blue glazed tiles is a six-meter-high M, a perforated, hollow structure lit from inside. Its "shadow" is dimly painted on the wooden trellis. The viewer perceives this sign depending on his or her position, the weather, and the light.

Restaurant with Kari Cavén's **The Flight of a Bat**

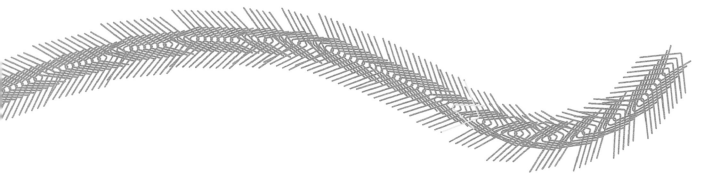

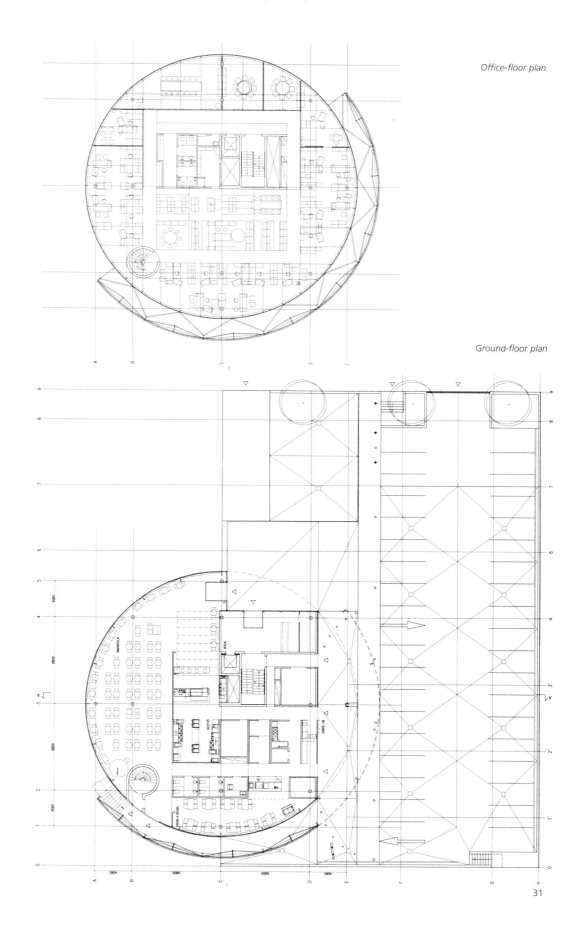

Office-floor plan

Ground-floor plan

ANGEL STUDIOS

Helsinki, Finland, 1997

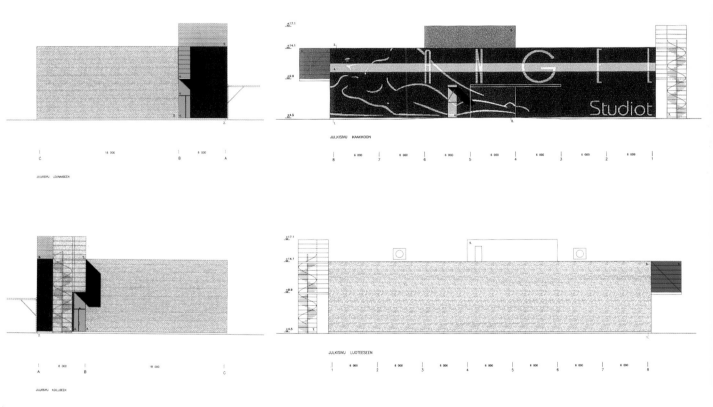

Study of elevations with corrugated-steel cladding

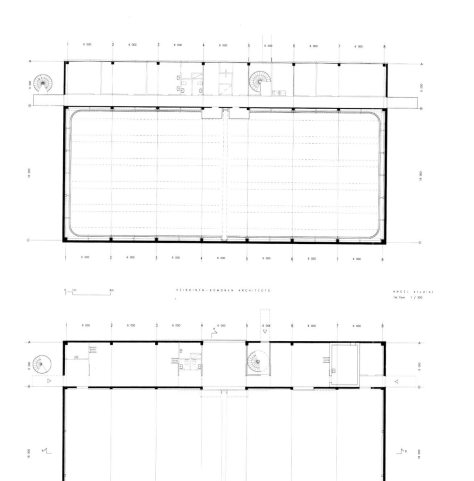

Mezzanine plan

Ground-floor plan

Located in an industrial suburb of Helsinki, Angel Studios provides rental space as well as equipment for film and video production companies. The rectangular volume consists of two sections. The studio portion, which may be divided by a retractable wall, abuts a unit containing offices, dressing rooms, workshops, and storage areas. The building's design conforms to the architectural character of the industrial surroundings. At the same time, its straightforwardness is ennobled by an ambitious and precise detailing of building elements. Offices are denoted by the uninterrupted horizontal flight of a strip window, for example, and the exit stairs are tightly dressed in zinc-coated steel mesh. The mechanical penthouse is a sharp-edged container covered in three-millimeter-thick butt-jointed aluminum plates.

The two sections of the box are distinguished by the finishes on the corrugated-steel cladding: matte-black and shiny, like camera film before and after exposure. The simple shed displays its corporate identity by means of the super-scaled firm logo painted across the building's facade.

AUDIOVISUAL CENTER FOR THE UNIVERSITY OF ART AND DESIGN

Helsinki, Finland, 1999

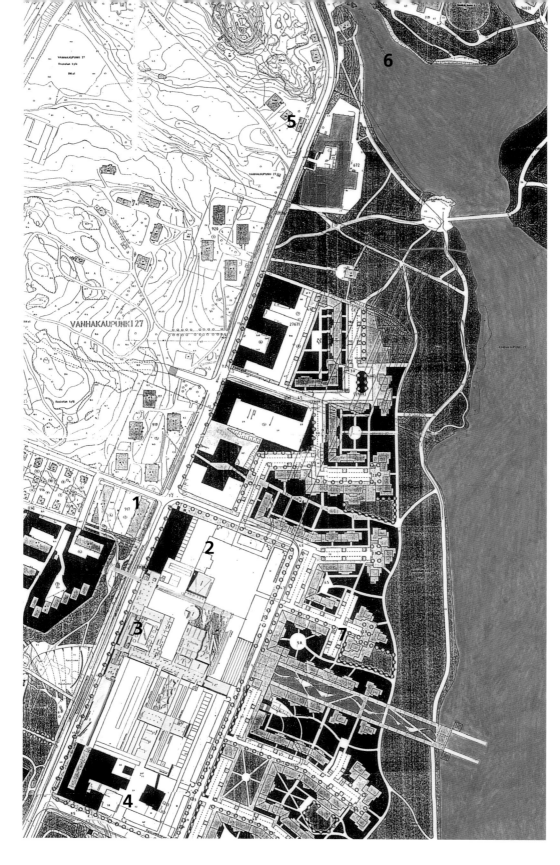

Arabianranta Design City: 1. University of Art and Design   2. Audiovisual Center   3. Hackmann Arabia Ceramics
4. Pop-Jazz Conservatory   5. School of Art and Communications   6. Museum of Technology   7. Housing

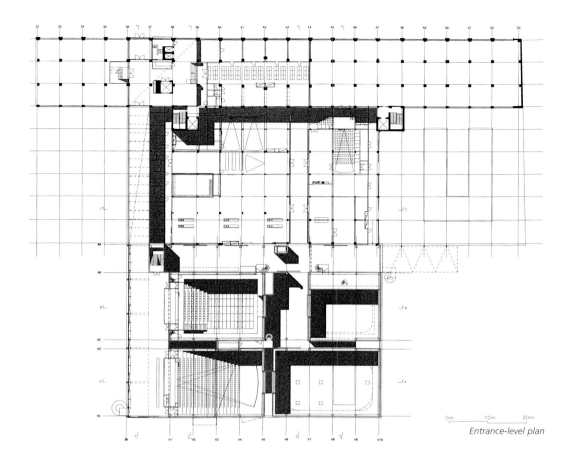

Entrance-level plan

The University of Art and Design is located in the old industrial premises of Arabia Ceramics in the historic section of Helsinki, where the city was founded in 1550. The area has a long tradition of industrial design manufacture. With ceramic production moving into modern technologies, vacant parts of the old factory buildings are available for new uses.

The Audiovisual Center will partly be incorporated into renovated manufacturing structures adjoining the existing University of Art and Design. Film and television studios, a black-box theater, and an auditorium will be located in a new addition.

The center is an integral part of a larger master plan for this industrial block. The extensive building complex projected can be seen as a small town, which will be organized hierarchically into squares and boulevards, back alleys and service areas. The renovation of the old manufacturing structure will retain its original roughness and authenticity, an approach that fits the practical needs of its new function.

The project includes rearranging the main entrance of the university as well. A glazed gallery connects the new entry across the block to the future main square of a proposed residential suburb. The gallery will have spaces for

exhibiting student projects and will also serve as the lobby for the four-hundred-seat auditorium and the experimental theater.

The Audiovisual Center implies numerous design layers of function and mechanical and electrical systems, as well as advanced cable networks. The architecture relies on a balanced coordination of these matrices. Its references are to microchips, in the sense of mastering complex flows of energy rather than of the fetishism of hardware icons.

45

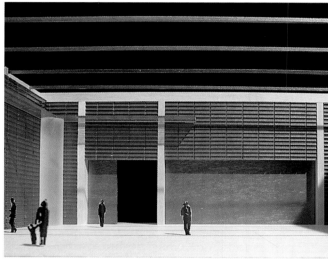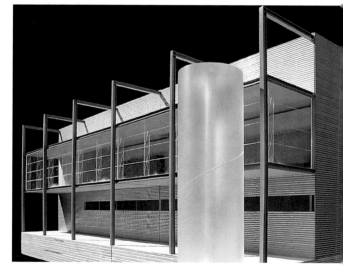

Clockwise from top left: Auditorium, film studio, gallery facade, gallery

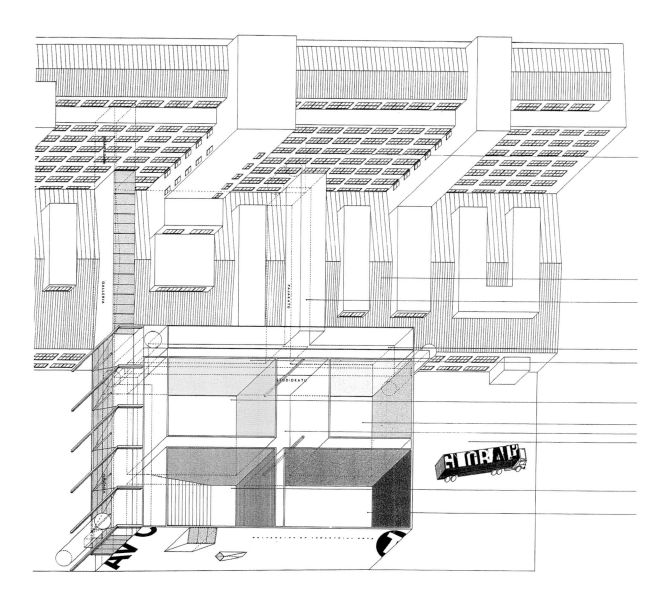

47

JOHNS HOPKINS UNIVERSITY STUDENT ART CENTER

Baltimore, Maryland, Competition, 1997

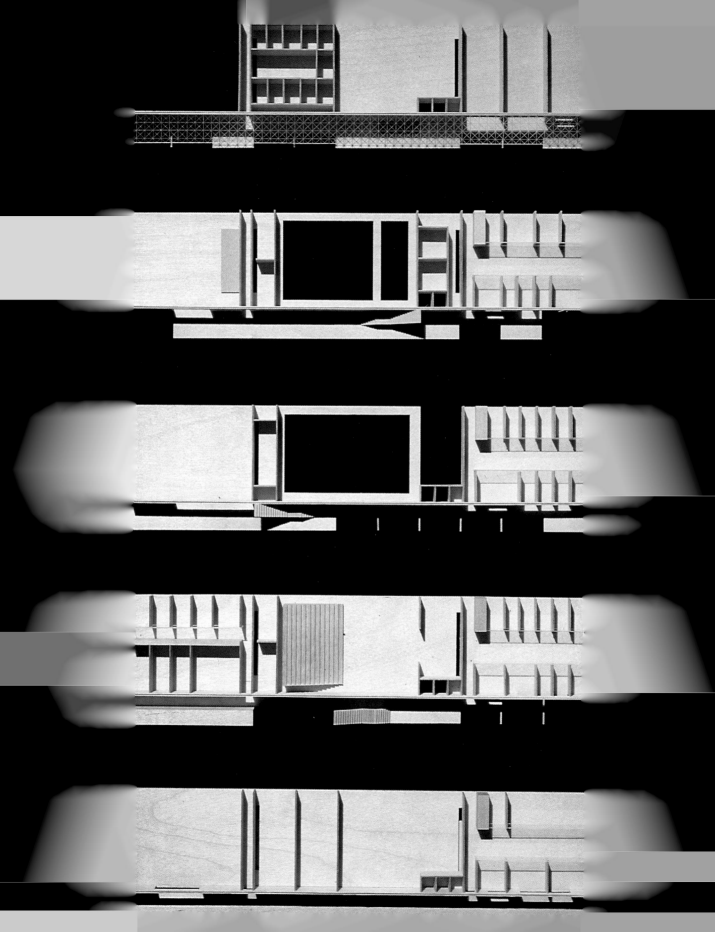

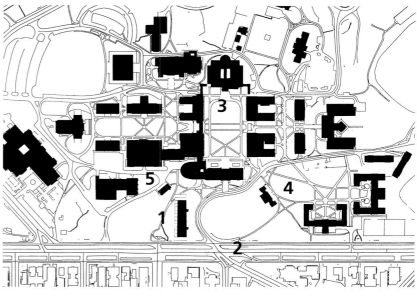

John Hopkins Campus: 1. Student Art Center   2. Charles Street
3. Eisenhower Library   4. Homewood House   5. Hopkins Theater

The new student art center building is integrated into the classical composition of the campus plan, serving as a link between Johns Hopkins University and the surrounding urban fabric of Baltimore. The building combines the aspects of the site: busy Charles Street and the beautiful park between Eisenhower Library and Hopkins Theater, a renovated old barn.

The footprint of the building has been designed to be as small as possible in order to avoid cutting down trees. The elongated structure is a simple container for the various parts of the art center: music, dance, film, and art studios; a black-box theater; and student offices. The glass-covered side gallery is a multilayered space as well as an indoor path from Charles Street to the campus. It also provides platforms and stages for random encounters.

The opposite ends of the gallery provide two different entrance plazas for the center. The entrance from Charles Street is equipped with an "info-wall," a screen advertising events going on in the building. The entrance from the campus is furnished with a pergola structure that supports fabric canopies and climbing plants, creating an outdoor meeting place in the park.

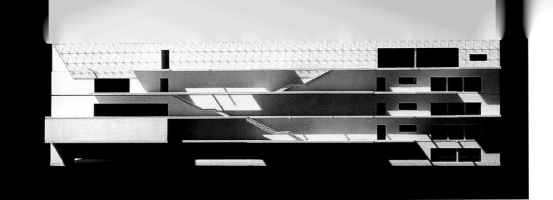

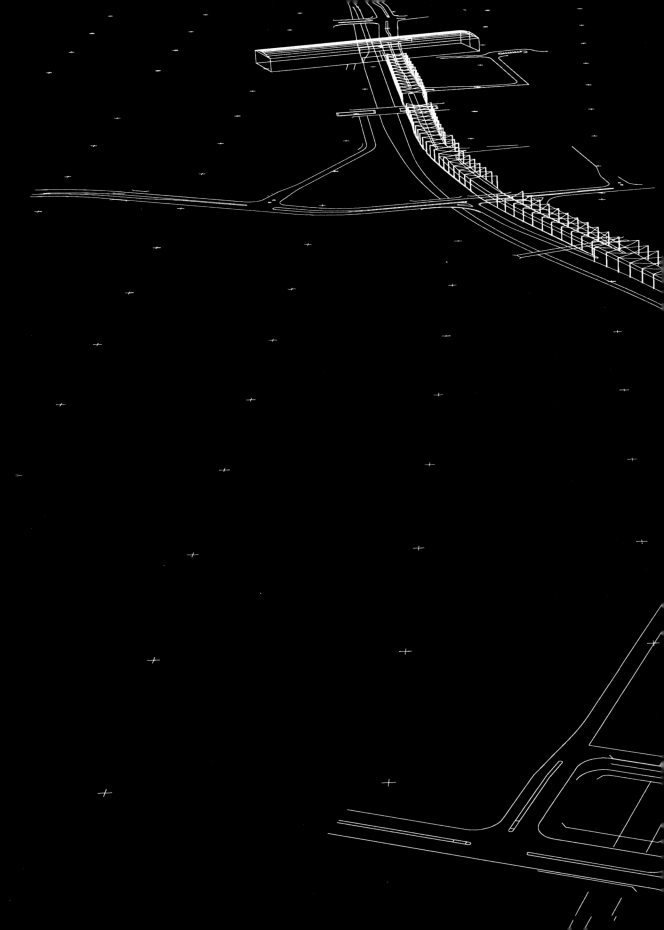

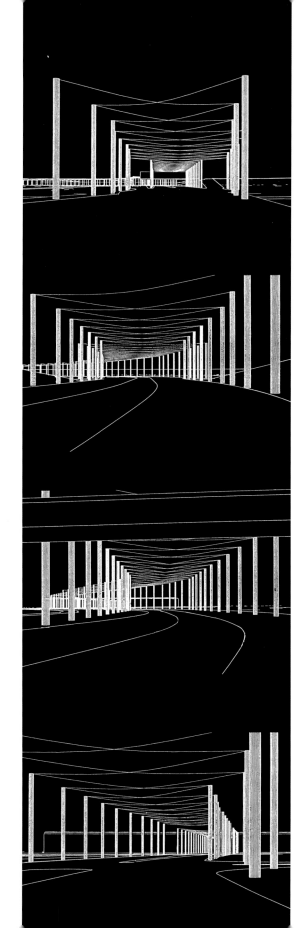

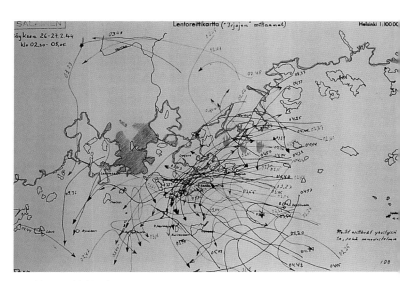

Air raids on Helsinki, February 26–27, 1944

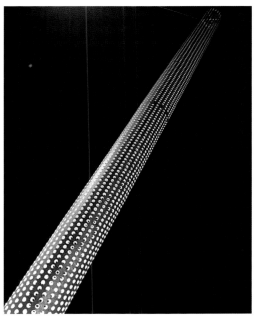

Test column

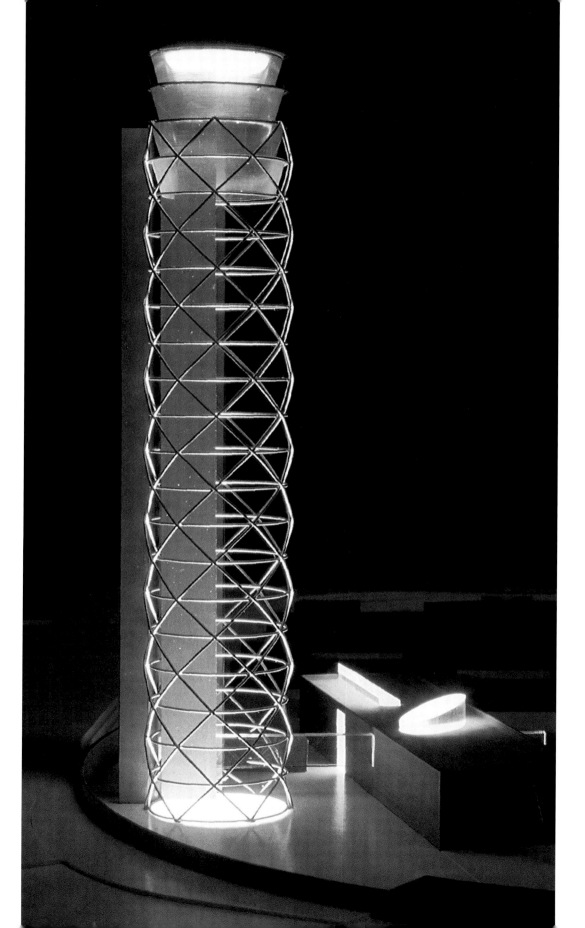

ARLANDA AIR-TRAFFIC CONTROL CENTER

Stockholm, Sweden, Competition, 1995

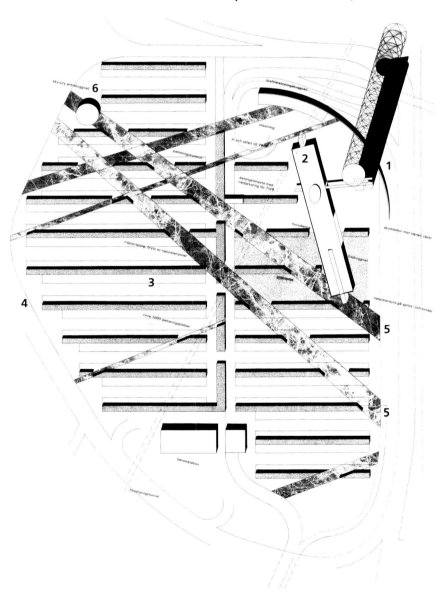

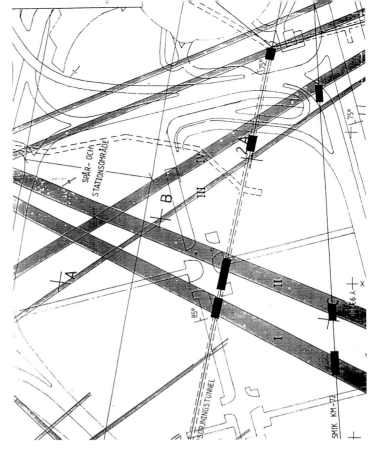

Geological map of site indicating underground cracks in the bedrock

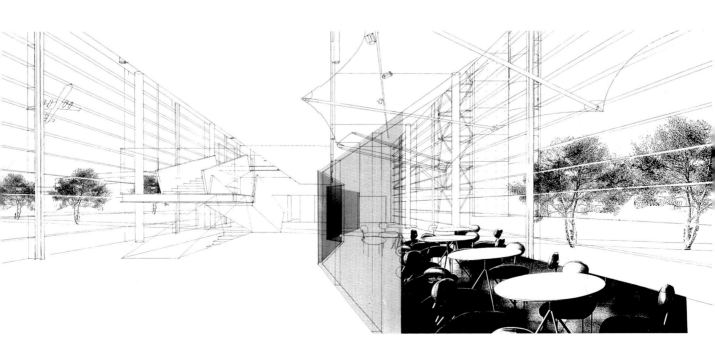

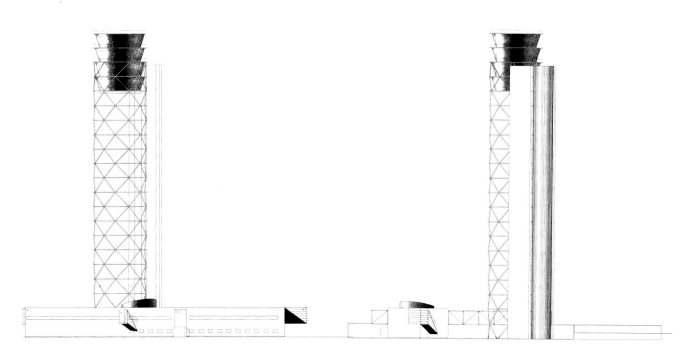

West elevation   *South elevation*

The Arlanda tower combines an open tubular steel grid supporting glazed control cabs with solid staircase, elevator, and service shafts, which are all structurally integrated. The 240-foot-high tower will be able to oversee the proposed third runway of the airport. This new vertical landmark is connected at ground level to a slim horizontal volume contain-ing support facilities like offices and service spaces.

Rearranging the surrounding parking area was a part of the project. The vast lot is structured by patterns of green and gray stripes. The green stripes are formed by hedges and indicate automobile parking spaces. The random gray zones embedded in asphalt are made of stone and reflect underground cracks in the bedrock above which it was not possible to locate the tower or other major structures. The relief of parallel and diagonal stripes is intended to create a kinetic inter-play visible from the road enter-ing the airport as well as from the air.

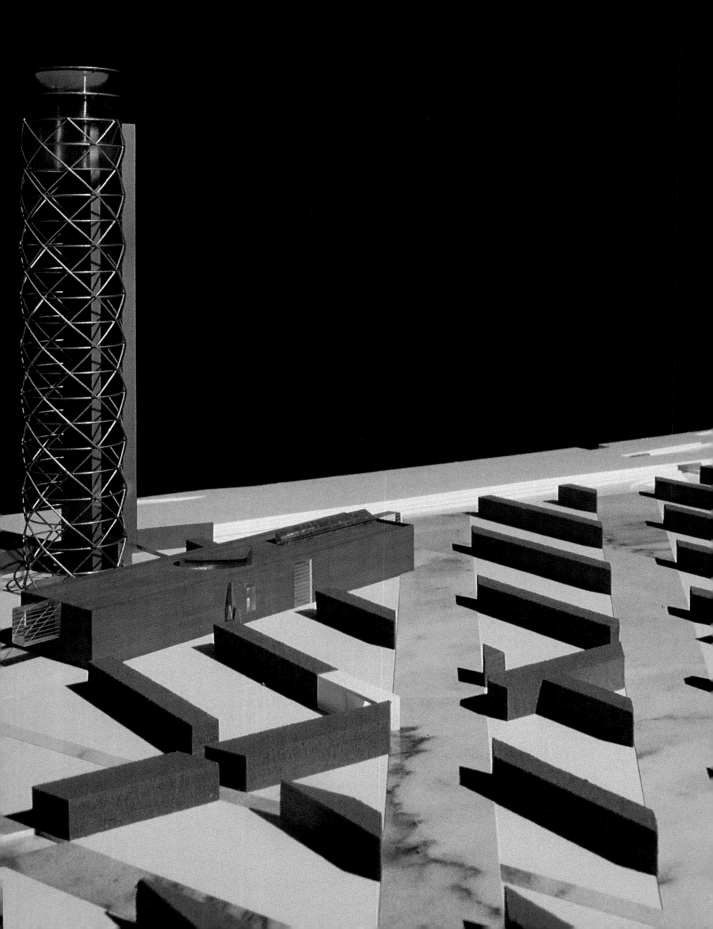

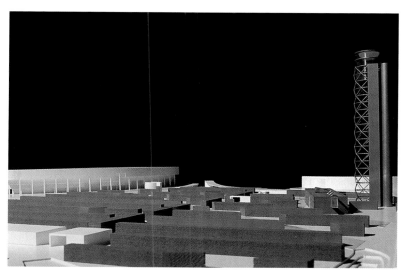

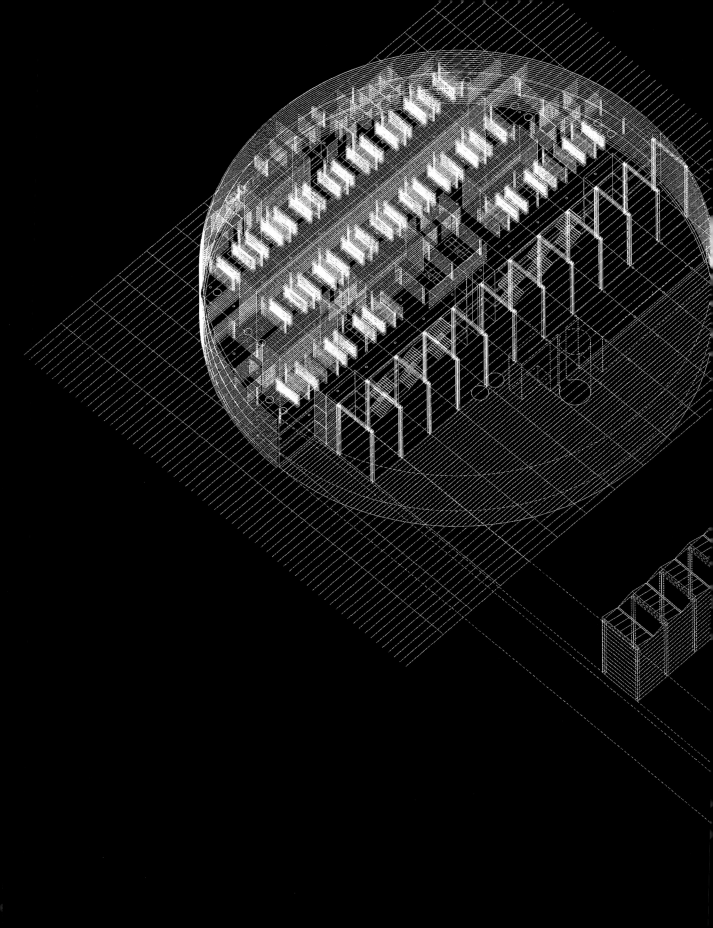

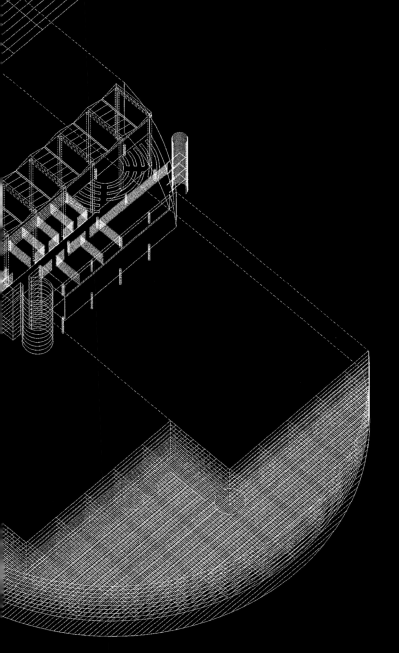

INFOCENTER FOR
VIIKKI SCIENCE PARK

Helsinki, Finland, Competition, 1996

π

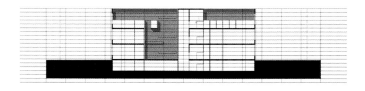

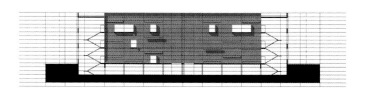

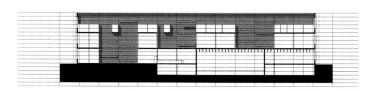

Sections

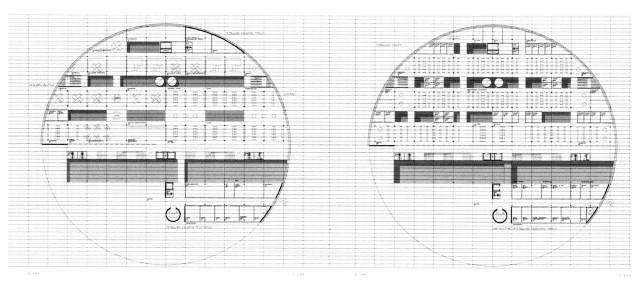

Second- and third-floor plans

Site plan

The Infocenter is sited at an intersection of roads, highways, and future tramlines, as well as at the axes and coordinates of many buildings in the area. The circular volume serves all these aspects equally, and the structure can be identified from all directions.

The central plaza of Viikki Science Park penetrates the circular form; the outdoor and the indoor create the whole. The plaza is planted with full-size linden trees whose foliage has been shaped to finish the cylindrical volume of the building. The facade itself is covered by oxidized copper mesh, which filters excessive sunlight. It creates a kinetic impression; depending on the angle from which it is viewed, it appears either impenetrable or completely transparent.

The Infocenter contains a public library on the ground floor and scientific libraries for the Helsinki University Biocenter on the subsequent two levels. The plan is organized within a rectilinear grid. The deep frame gets light through three-story greenhouses, which form an oasis in the staccato of the vast library landscape. These glazed boxes are an integral part of the metabolic system of the building. They might house Mediterranean or tropical jungle plant life. Their surplus heat helps warm the Infocenter during the winter.

TEBOIL RAJAHOVI
SERVICE STATION

Vaalimaa, Finland, 1996

Site plan

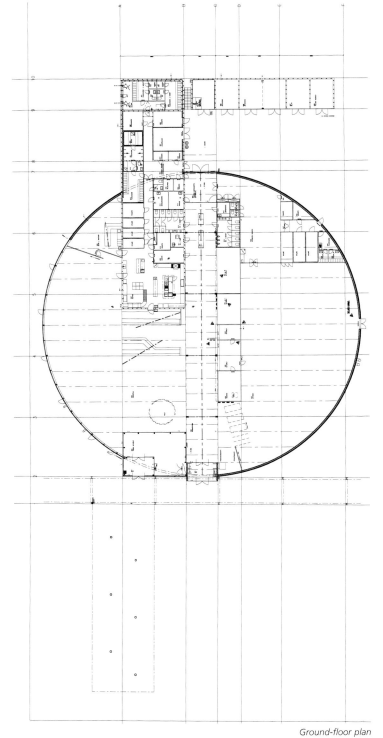

Ground-floor plan

As recently as twenty years ago, service-station chains in Finland were easily distinguishable from one another. Although the buildings themselves, all based on standardized plans, resembled one another, they merely formed a neutral backdrop for the striking advertising graphics of companies such as Gulf, Shell, and Esso. Today filling stations have evolved into multiservice centers that all look the same with their colorful structures competing for the soul of the postmodern motorist.

Ribbon-cutting speeches refer to these marketplaces as landmarks, calling cards, or even flagships of their locality. But the pursuit of originality finds itself in a certain tension with the actual function of the building: the challenge is to produce a design that is simultaneously eye-catching yet flexible and efficient—a matrix of overlapping vehicular, service,

and passenger traffic networks. Teboil Rajahovi is situated in Vaalimaa, the busiest gateway between Finland and Russia: in 1995 nearly 1.4 million passengers and more than a half million vehicles (including 190,000 trucks) passed through the checkpoint.

The structure is composed of a flat steel cylinder that presents a similar image to travelers in both directions along the road. The facade is made of 2.5-millimeter-thick steel plates, which are fastened with open joints to corrugated weatherproof sheeting. The blue-enamel-finished surface can appear translucent or can act as a mirror reflecting the lights and shades of the surrounding environment. A glass-roofed internal corridor divides the building into two sections: a market on one side and a restaurant and filling station area on the other. Apart from the kitchen,

rest rooms, and technical facilities, which are gathered together inside a concrete-framed container, the structure forms an open hall. The interior of the hall is dominated by the ceiling, whose structural latticework and utility installation systems provide a counterpoint for the pluralistic floorscape of furnishings chosen by the client.

The building's simple form is enhanced by an extensive canopy structure, which also serves as scaffolding for advertisements. Prosaic advertising fittings can often ruin a sensitive composition. At Teboil Rajahovi an important aim from the outset was the integration of architecture and commercial graphics in order to produce a disciplined whole. The light boxes, neon tubes, and logos are every bit as much a part of the facade as the details on the canopy tension rods.

Health Center, Mali, Guinea

ELEMENTARY STRUCTURES

Guinea, 1994–

Villa Eila, Mali, Guinea

Health Center: section and views

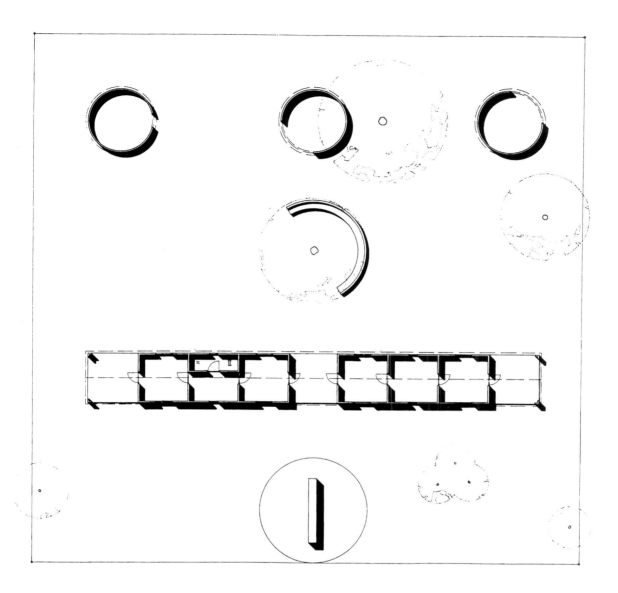

Health Center: plan

Several small buildings were designed for aid programs directed by the Finland-based Indigo Foundation in the villages of Guinea in West Africa. The first building, realized in 1994, was a health center, and was followed by a villa in 1995, two primary schools in 1997, and a training center for chicken farmers in 1998.

The technical premise for all these buildings is the use of stabilized earth blocks instead of kiln-fired bricks, the making of which poses a danger to the forests. Depending on the local conditions, timber or bamboo is used for roof structures. The roofing itself is made of straw, three-millimeter-thick cement tiles reinforced with fiber, or, occasionally, corrugated metal. Electricity is produced by solar panels.

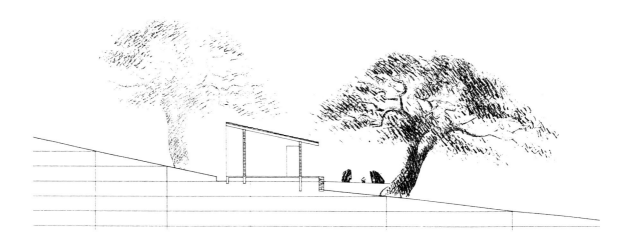

Villa Eila: section, plan, and views

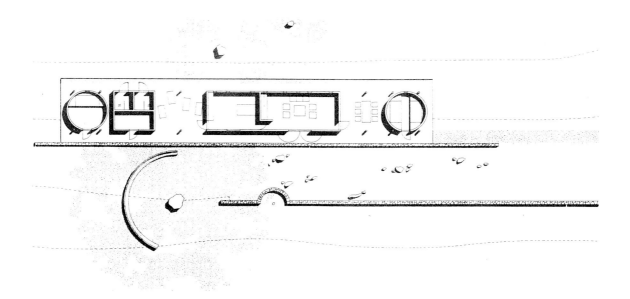

MEDIA CENTER

Helsinki, Finland, Competition, 1995

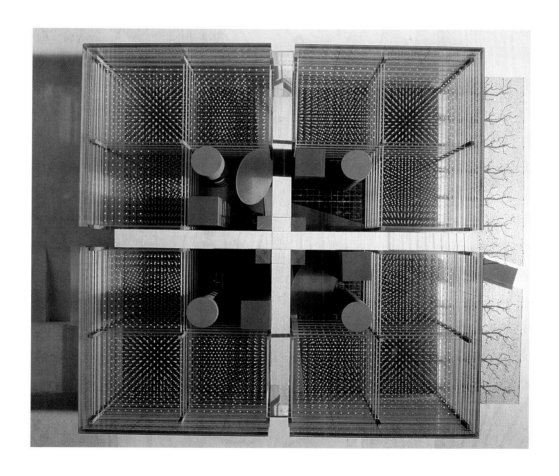

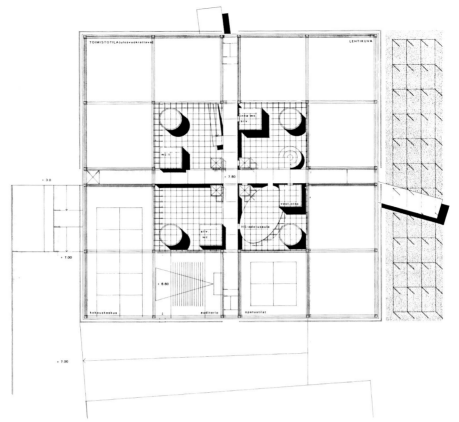

Typical floor plan

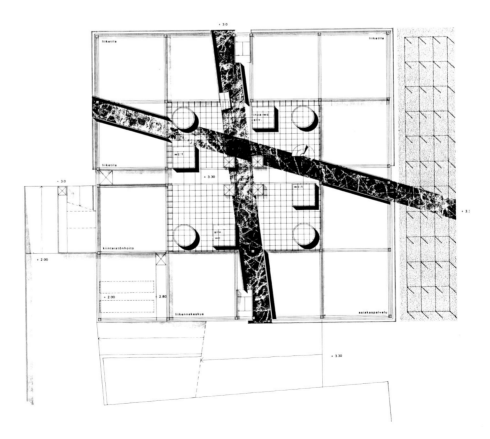

Ground-floor plan

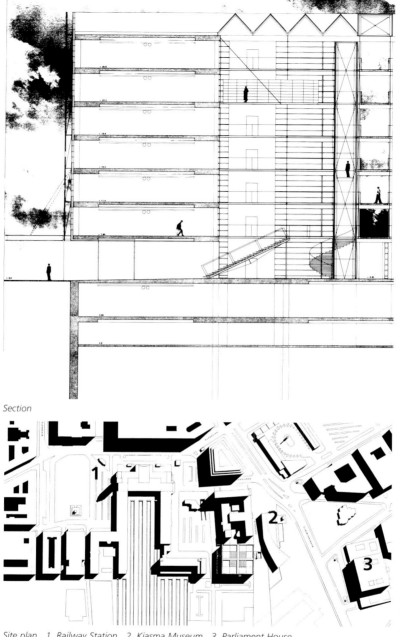

Section

Site plan   1. Railway Station   2. Kiasma Museum   3. Parliament House

Located in the center of Helsinki, the building is the new headquarters for *Helsingin Sanomat*, the country's largest newspaper. The cubic volume is covered on the exterior with a sunshading grille made of oxidized bronze. The facade behind the grille is finished with dark blue steel and glass. The blue color is visible only when the facade is viewed straight on; from other angles the building discloses only the greenish color of its bronze veil.

The office spaces are organized around a skylit hall that contains staircases, elevators, bridges, balconies, and conference rooms. The almost Piranesian complexity of the hall balances the horizontal layers of the office landscapes, which are structured to coordinate with the mechanical, electrical, and functional systems.

EMERGENCY SERVICES COLLEGE

Kuopio, Finland, 1992, 1995

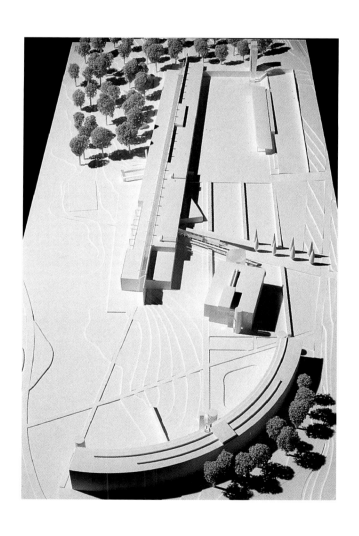

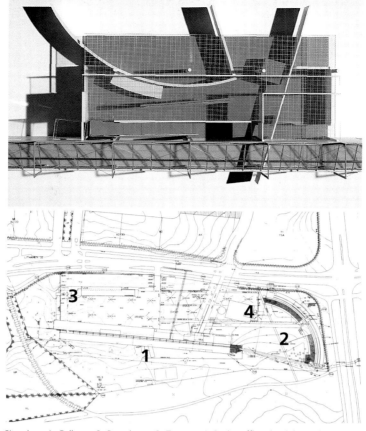

Site plan   1. College   2. Dormitory   3. Towers   4. Senior officers' training unit

The college prepares firefighters and rescue personnel to cope with disasters. A clear and compact spatial layout provides framework for a training program that is intended to develop confidence, promptness, prudence, and resolution—the bases of the required professional skills.

The campus consists of a college building that includes a firehouse, a senior officers' training unit, and a dormitory. A glass-covered corridor, more than two hundred meters long, runs through the main building, structuring the various functions of the institution and connecting the classrooms to the garage for fire and rescue vehicles so that they are clearly visible in all parts of the building.

Two towers for drying fire hoses and practicing rescue operations form a backdrop for Pyörö Boulevard. From the open roof terrace of the school it is possible to watch training sessions and demonstrations.

The senior officers' training unit was built as a later addition to the original design. To maximize the limited space provided by the site, the program was packed into a four-story container. The sandblasted glass-block cylinder contains the main vertical arteries, creating coherence between the floors and articulating the exterior.

The curved dormitory opens out like a stage toward the school. Each morning it gives a "performance" as 350 students rush to their classes along the side galleries, which are covered by chain-link fencing. Above the main building's glazed skylight hangs a lighting beam that illuminates the central passage and is a beacon for the neighborhood.

The design of the project was inspired by a fifteenth-century guide to Japanese swordsmanship, *A Book of Five Rings*, written by the legendary samurai Miyamoto Musashi.

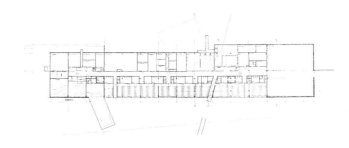

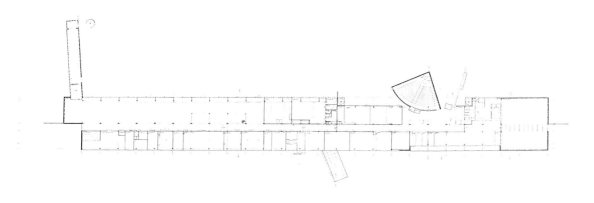

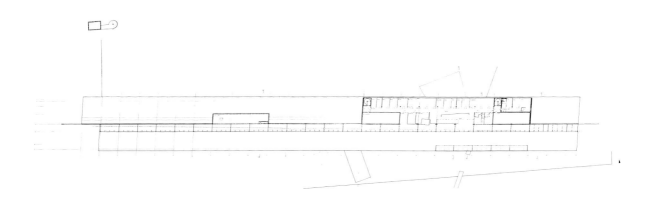

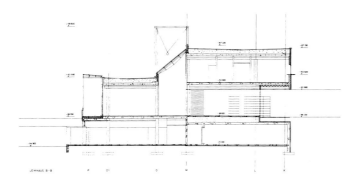

College: plans and sections

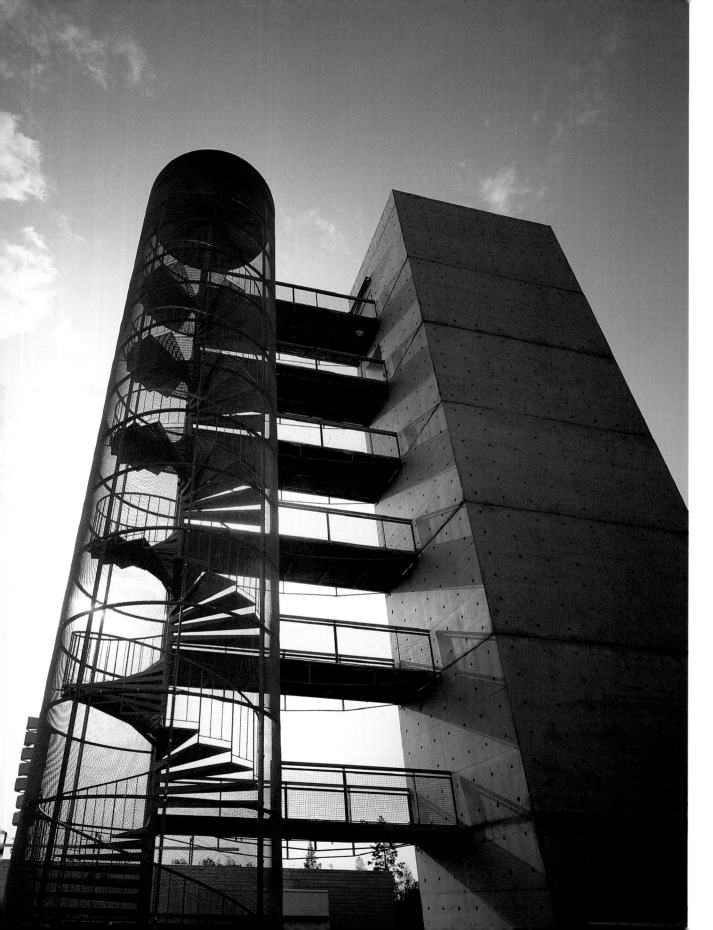

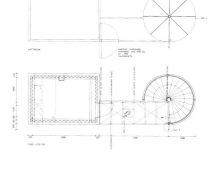

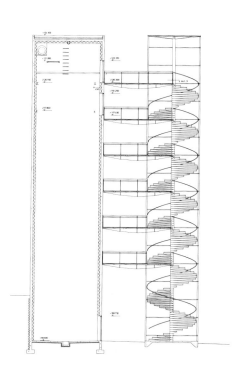

College: tower plans and tower section

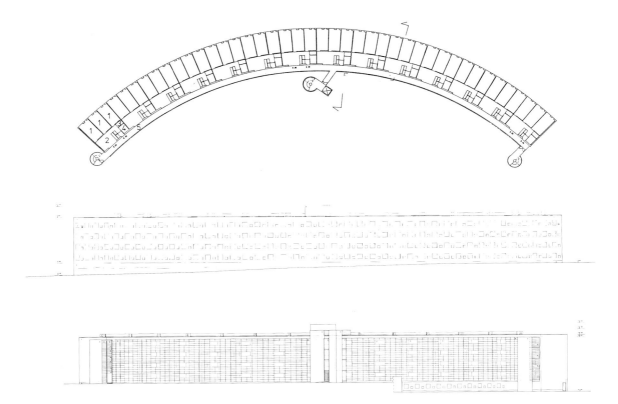

Dormitory: typical plan and elevations

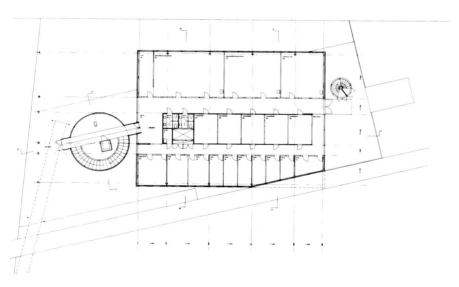

Senior officers' training unit: typical plan

FOIBE SENIOR CITIZEN HOUSING AND AMENITY CENTER

Vantaa, Finland, 1994

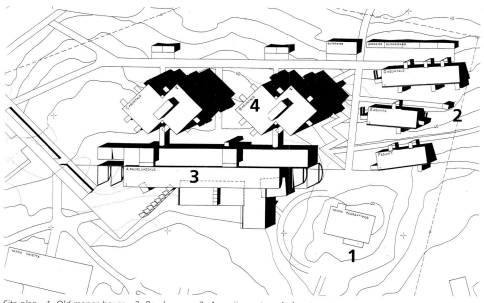

Site plan 1. Old manor house 2. Rowhouses 3. Amenity center 4. Apartments

Like the unchanging patterns for dollhouses and gingerbread cottages, homes for both the young and the old have been limited to uncreative stereotypes. The standard (Scandinavian) recipe for children's spaces calls for overly busy, dwarf-scaled structures and spaces—a kind of postmodern apotheosis. Meanwhile, the elderly are often confined to Jane Austen–style settings, of the sort commonly found in open-air museums.

Senior citizens today are more heterogeneous than ever before. The architecture for a mature population must serve the universal experience of the slowing pace of life, but it need not be preoccupied with creating romanticized images of what "leisure living" should be. Architecture's response to aging entails more than merely the provision of handrails, technical appliances, and services or electrical systems. When the radius of one's daily territory is reduced, one's dwelling must change to meet totally new demands. Is the television the only window to the outside world? The entry, the corridor, and the stairway no longer mark the unconscious distance from the home to the car, but grow to form a whole city for the resident. How does one enjoy an entire day within the confines of an apartment? How will the home accommodate the need to receive friends or help, when wanted or necessary? In other words, how does the private meet the public?

At Foibe there is always more than one view to contemplate; rooms in the corners of the crystal-like building open perpendicularly in two directions to allow the sun to shine in most of the day. The journey from each resident's front door begins in a semiprivate enclosure furnished by the resident and his or her nearest neighbors. Next is the semipublic section of the floor, where the communal stair and the elevator are located. The arterial road of the building leads to a glazed corridor, across a Japanese garden, and to the service center. The saunas, gyms, swimming pool, arts and crafts rooms, restaurant, and library are grouped in colorful "buildings" along the main hall, creating the scale of a small village.

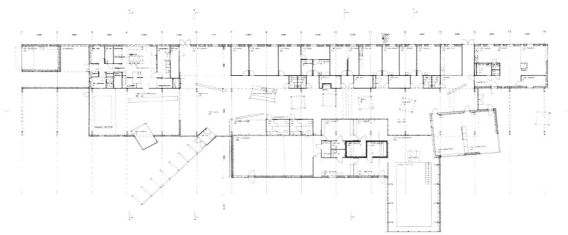

Amenity center: ground-floor plan

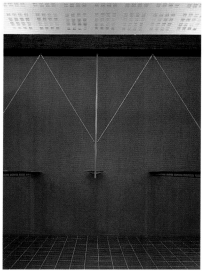

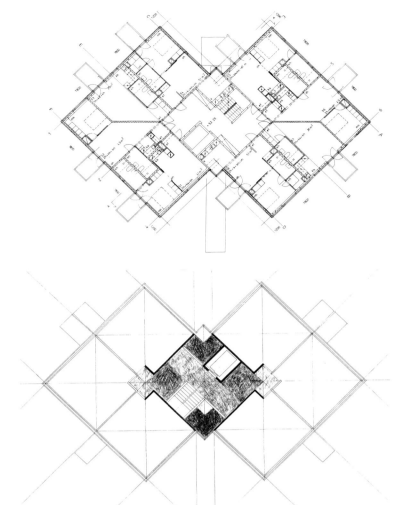

Apartments: ground-floor plan and typical floor plan

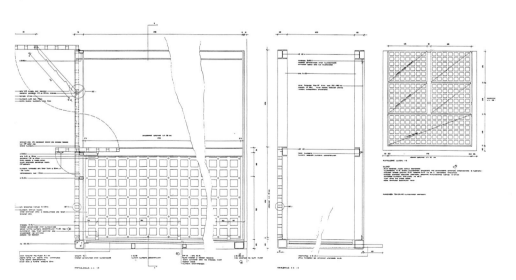

Apartments: balcony details

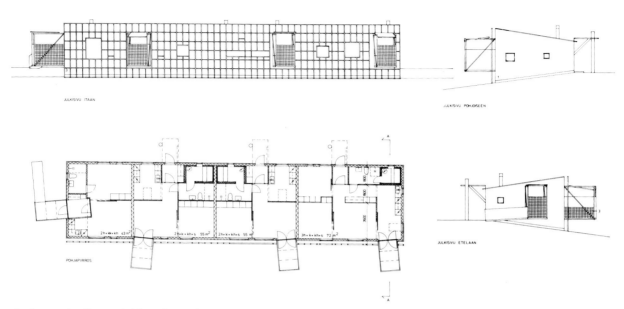

JULKISIVU ITÄÄN

JULKISIVU POHJOISEEN

POHJAPIIRROS

2h+kk+kh 63m²   2h+k+kh+s 55 m²   2h+k+kh+s 55 m²   3h+k+kh+s 72 m²

JULKISIVU ETELÄÄN

Rowhouses: elevations, typical floor plan, section

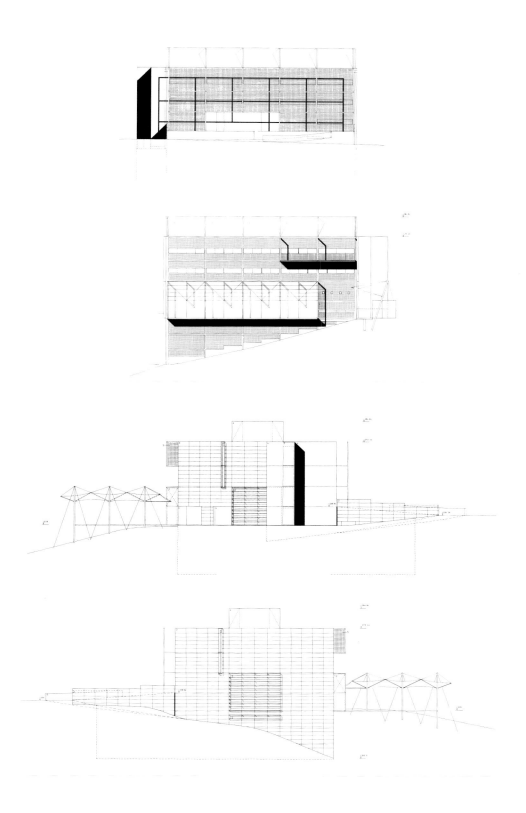

Office-floor plan

123

MODULAR EXHIBITION PAVILION FOR MARIMEKKO

1993 – 96

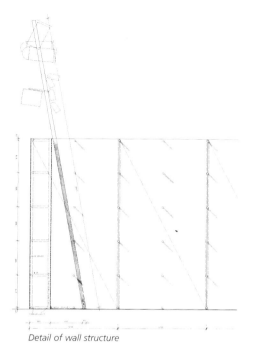

Detail of wall structure

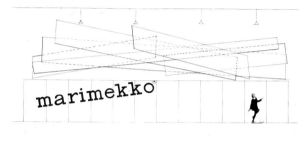

Elevation

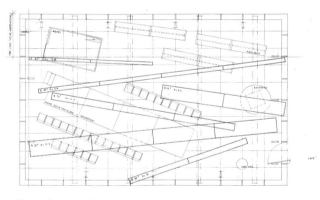

Plan

Plan with alternative sail set-up

The modular pavilion was used to exhibit Marimekko products at fairs in Düsseldorf, Frankfurt, Paris, Copenhagen, Stockholm, and Helsinki. The structural system is based on transportable elements from which pavilions of different sizes and shapes can be built to meet varying display needs.

The freestanding wall elements are made of two gray, perforated steel plates with structure in between. The elements appear solid when viewed at an angle, but translucent when seen head on. The overlapping perforations produce a moiré effect, which is strengthened by floodlights between the plates; the patterns change as the viewer moves.

The door of the pavilion, platform, coat racks, and storage units are of thick gray-stained plywood. The cocktail table is a red granite disk. Suspended above the pavilion is a white sail whose asymmetrical wing shape serves as Marimekko's signpost in the exhibition hall.

EUROPEAN FILM COLLEGE

Ebeltoft, Denmark, 1993

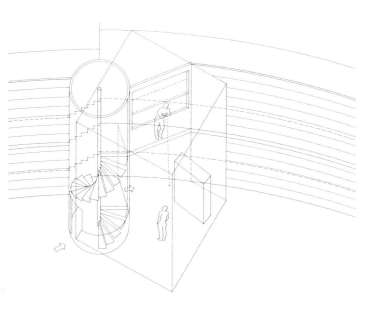

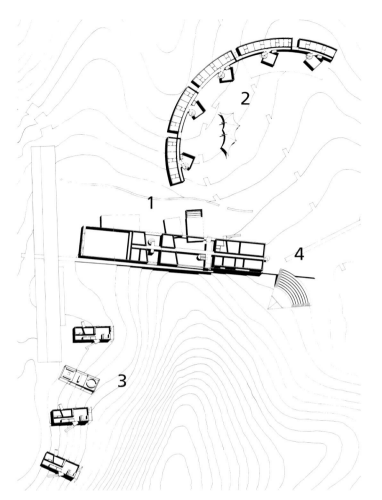

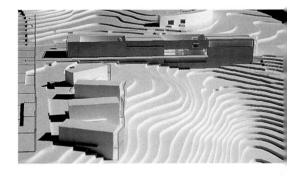

Site plan   1. School   2. Dormitory   3. Teachers' houses   4. Outdoor auditorium

The European Film College is a part of the traditional Danish *Folkehöjskole* program, which provides popular education without formal degrees. It is a boarding school that teaches film to movie lovers of all ages but also offers short-term courses for professionals.

The site is a green field near the picturesque city center of Ebeltoft. The complex comprises the school, student dormitory, and faculty residences. The school houses two movie theaters, studios, workshops, classrooms, administrative facilities, and a restaurant.

The main building cuts the site in two; the deep valley created by the Ice Age was left untouched, but the courtyard facing the dormitory is planned for gatherings. The southern facade, containing storage areas, kitchen, and studios, re-creates the scale of a small Danish town or the first film studios in 1920s Copenhagen, while the northern facade, clad in three-millimeter-thick zinc-coated steel plating, has a more austere character.

The entrance to the college is via a long and narrow bridge, cantilevered high above the valley and facing the skyline of the town and nearby bay. (Any resemblance to Hitchcock's *Vertigo* is purely coincidental.)

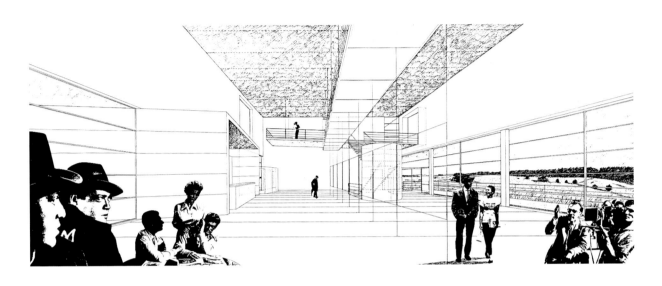

134

Section

137

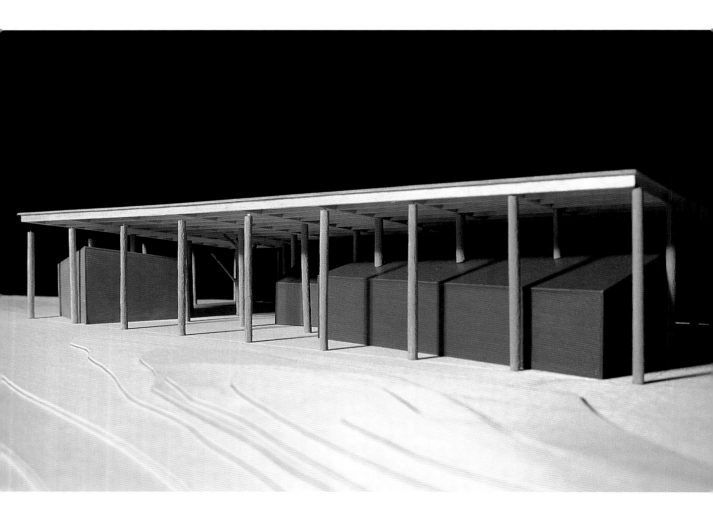

CENTERS FOR KARELIAN CULTURE

Kuhmo, Finland / Kostamus, Russia
Project, 1993

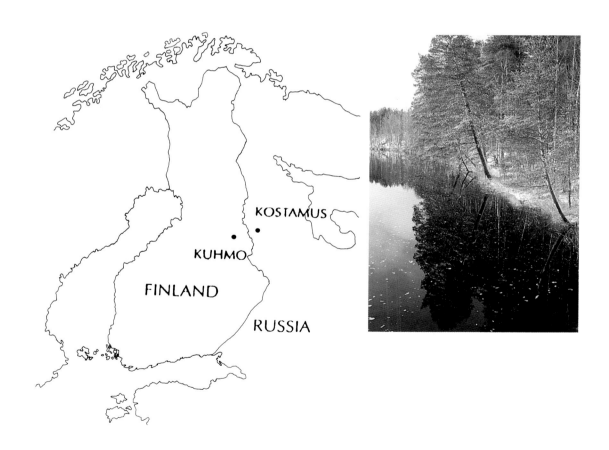

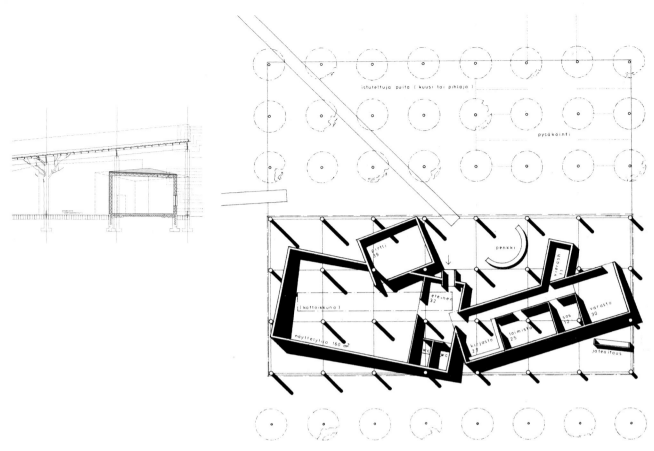

Kuhmo: section and plan

Kostamus: plan

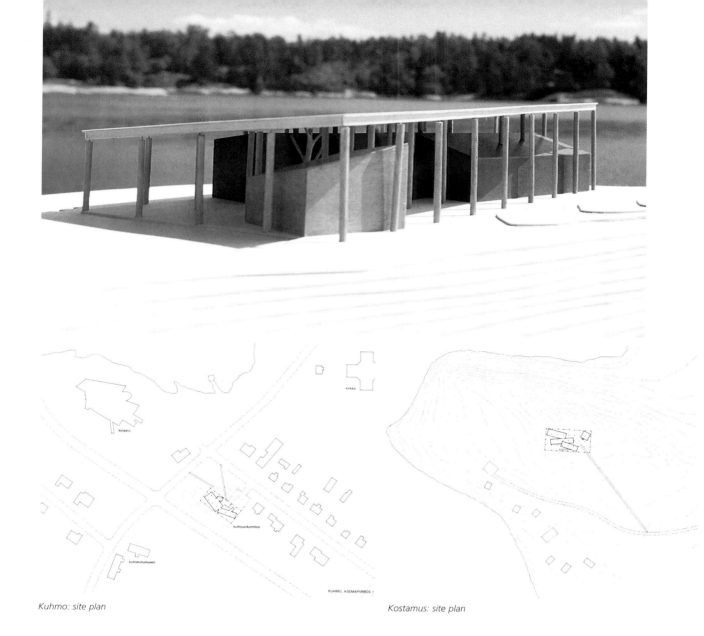

Kuhmo: site plan

Kostamus: site plan

These two institutions collect documents and provide information for visitors to the villages of Karelian, the region where the songs of *Kalevala* were chanted and where it is still possible to hear archaic Finnish spoken and sung.

Kalevala, the national epic of Finland, was published nearly 150 years ago, when the tradition of epic singing was still alive and well in Karelian villages. *Kalevala* became the cornerstone of Finnish language and cultural mythology but also the model for *Hiawatha*.

The pavilion buildings vary in response to local conditions of site and program; nevertheless, each contains exhibition spaces, a library, an office, and a workshop, and they are linked to each other in terms of design. In both, stable log pillars carry a vast, slightly tilted grass roof that covers a small "village" of wooden cottages and shelters a private outdoor area.

MATRIX H₂O MADRID

Madrid, Spain, Exhibition, 1992

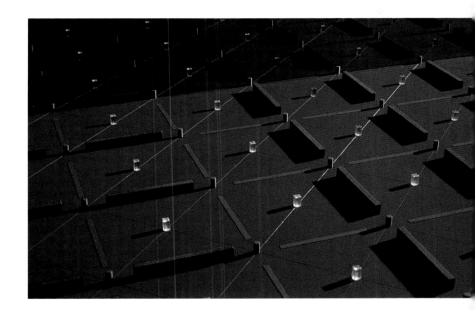

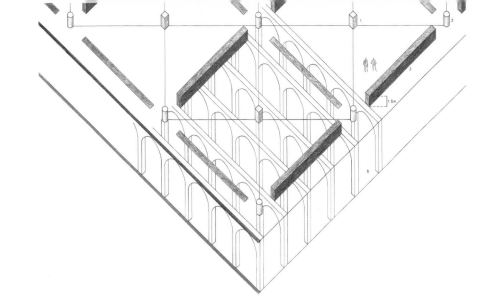

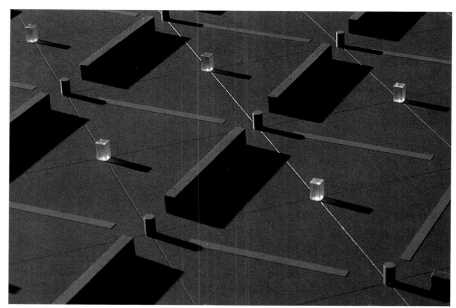

Section through water pillar

A few anonymous vacant spaces on the outskirts of the urban fabric of Madrid reveal an important story: the withered grass conceals the city's underground water reservoirs. Madrid uses six hundred liters of water per person per day, requiring rich natural resources and complicated technical systems. Turning on a tap to obtain water is taken for granted; the user seldom considers how it is delivered or the fact that pure drinking water has become a commodity more valuable than oil.

Historically, the value of water was directly visible in the built environment. The village well was a small monument and an important social meeting place.

The Roman aqueducts and even the water conduits constructed in Queen Isabella's time show how this vital liquid and its architecture were a conspicuous and important part of the environment. The etymology of the name of the city itself attests to the importance of water: "Madrid" comes from a word meaning "matrix," referring to the water distribution systems built by the Moors.

Matrix H_2O Madrid was a project for the exhibition "Visiones para Madrid" organized by the city. The fields covering the underground reservoirs are built up as a "matrix," establishing a monument to water and providing this peripheral and anonymous dis-

trict of the city with a story and genius loci. The matrix consists of square-based water towers, cylindrical ventilation columns, oblong hedges, and stripes of green grass, all set against the reddish sand. Its image will shift according to light, shadow, and viewpoint.

HOUSE OF CULTURE

Nuuk, Greenland, Competition, 1992

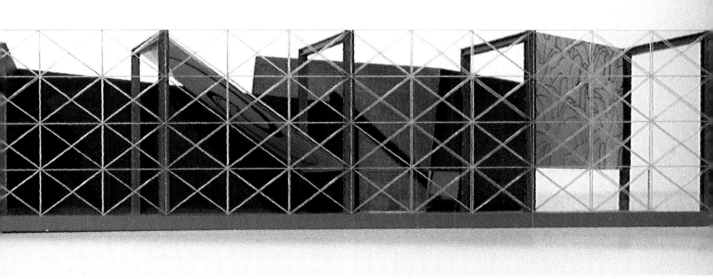

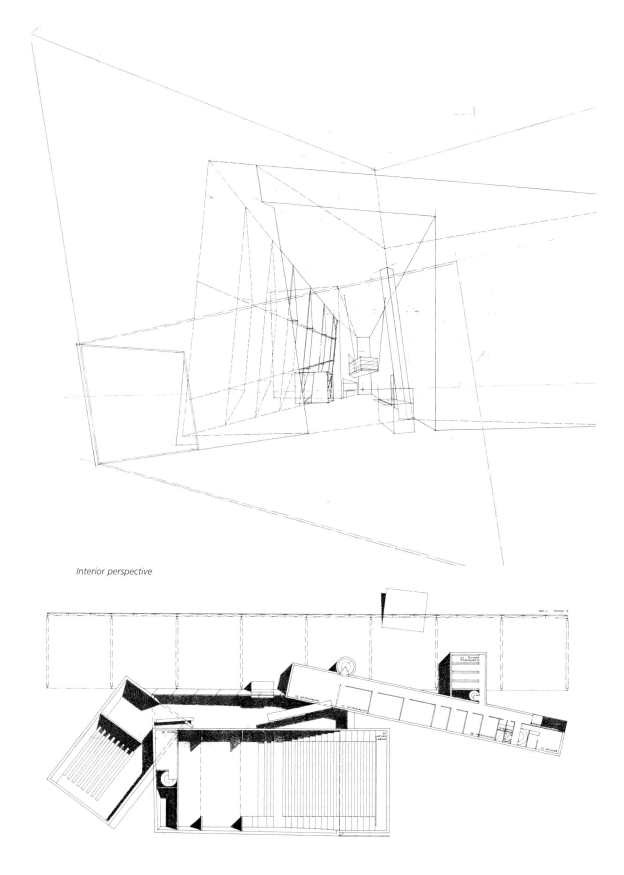

Interior perspective

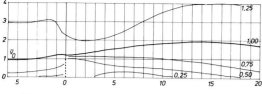
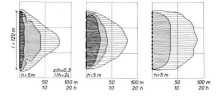

Wind diagrams

The cultural center creates a comfortable microclimate, converting the site, a leftover piece at the end of Skibhavnsvej, the main pedestrian street of Nuuk, into an urban public outdoor space, an active meeting point for the townspeople. The south-western side of what is essentially an outdoor foyer has a wall made of perforated steel that offers protection from winter storms. The strong, southerly summer winds are subdued with netlike sails fixed to the steel frames above street level.

The program consists of two multipurpose auditoriums, an art school, library, administrative facilities, and an entrance hall containing a cafeteria and exhibition facilities. Each of these functions is in an autonomous building volume that is integrated into the whole by means of the entrance foyer. The fragmented structure reflects the free-form urban composition of Nuuk and the dramatic slow motion of massive ice slabs breaking free from the mainland glacier.

AIRPORT TERMINAL
Rovaniemi, Finland, 1992

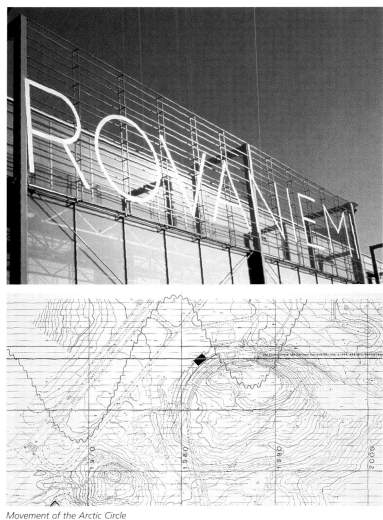

Movement of the Arctic Circle

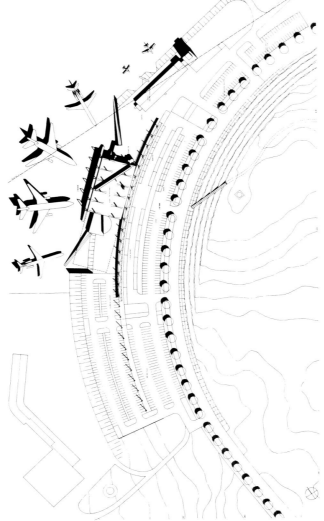

Site plan

An airport terminal is a filter for the flow of people, goods, and communication. Its functional complexity is increased today by exacting security regulations.

The design for the new passenger terminal is an iron container, a simple box with a minimum of inhibiting fixed structures. The building is integrated into its setting and the sweeping forms of the landscape with a 180-meter-long curved canopy. Roads, parking areas, and terraced rock follow the same environmental geometry.

The structure is given a cosmic context by two installations fused into the architecture. One is an oblique forty-meter-long skylight parallel to the meridian of the Arctic Circle. The polar meridian coincided with this aperture most recently during the design of the building, in 1990. The next pass through the opening is projected in 47954 A.D.

A second installation, designed by the artist Lauri Anttila, is called *Orbit of the Earth*. Each day the spot of light projected through the ceiling by the noon sun is in a different position. The pattern formed by these spots in the course of a year makes an elongated figure eight, the analemma of the sun, which is a projection of the elliptical orbit of the earth.

These two simple cosmic instruments integrated in the harsh functional building provide a kind of counter narrative to the popular image of the city as the home base of Santa Claus.

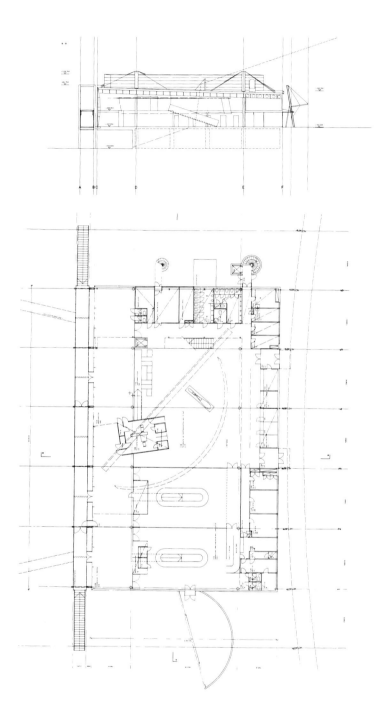

The Orbit of the Earth *by Lauri Anttila*   *Section, plan*

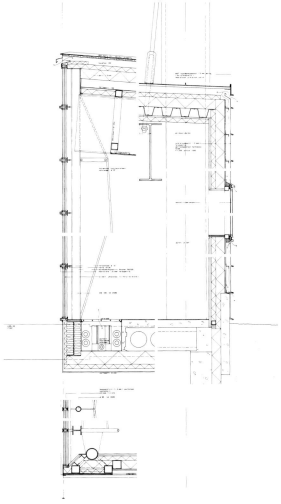

Sections

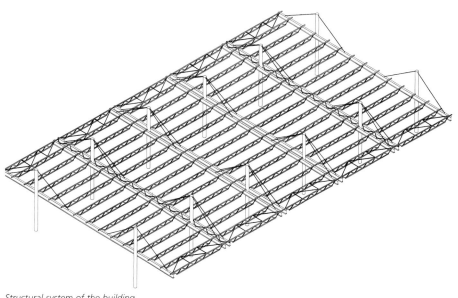

Structural system of the building

FINNISH PAVILION
FOR A NORDIC ART
AND ARCHITECTURE
EXHIBITION

Leeuwarden, The Netherlands
1990

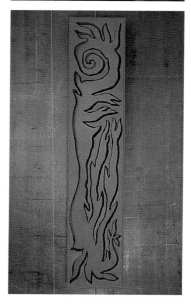

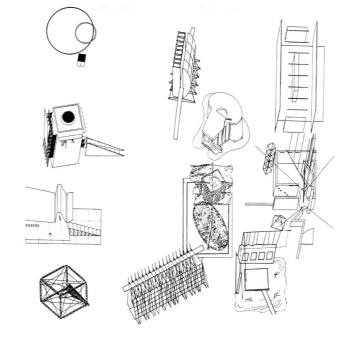

Axonometric of exhibition layout

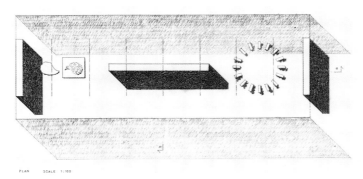

Axonometric of pavilion

The exhibition "11 Cities 11 Nations: Contemporary Nordic Art and Architecture" was organized to explore Northern European cultural identity and the links between architecture and the visual arts. Ten artists and architects from the cities of Reykjavik, Dublin, Edinburgh, Hamburg, Oslo, Copenhagen, Stockholm, Gdansk, Tallinn, and Helsinki were invited to participate.

The basic premise of the pavilion was to create visual "acoustics" that would carve from the huge diversity of forms in the exhibition hall a distinct territory for the works of the Finnish sculptor Martti Aiha. Six-meter-high sheets of steel mesh suspended from the roof of the hall form the side walls of the exhibition area. Seen from outside, the walls of the strongly lit cage are transparent; inside the pavilion, against the dark hall, the mesh creates a solid-looking wall that defines the space. The sculptures are attached to five-millimeter-thick steel slabs whose untreated hot-rolled surface offers a strong textural background that appears to shift from deep black to turquoise blue.

HEUREKA
FINNISH SCIENCE CENTER
Vantaa, Finland, 1988

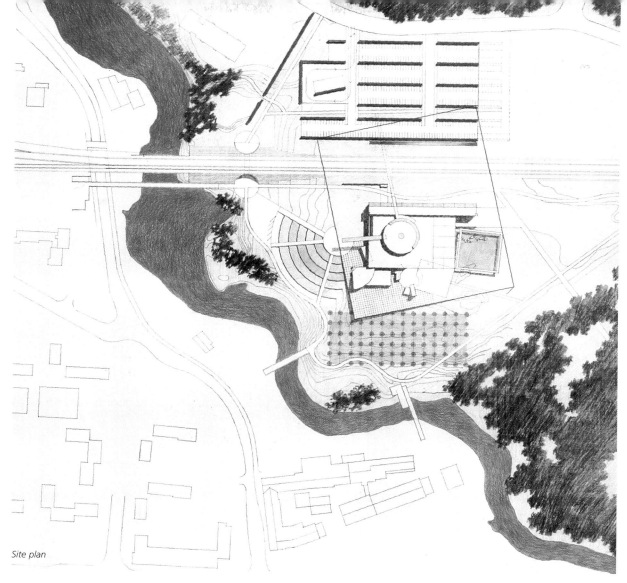

Site plan

The Science Center is located at the junction of the busiest railway line in Finland and the Kerava River, a cultural landscape that has a rich history dating back to the Bronze Age. An agglomeration of concrete, steel, and wooden constructions contains an auditorium, classrooms, and a combined planetarium and wide-screen cinema. For each architectural element, an appropriate structural system was developed.

The design of the Science Center refers to the contradictory dynamics of nature itself, forces seeking order and balance countered by disruptive and chaotic tendencies. Scientific analyses and demonstrations of natural phenomena have been integrated into the architectural and landscaping themes. The reflective glass facade facing the railway line is an acoustical shield against noise from the trains; its steel structure displays the color spectrum of visible light. The stone garden that dominates the entryway to the building re-creates Finland's geological map, reflecting the long cycle of nature.

The name of the center, Heureka, was derived from the code name of the competition entry. Together with the Archimedean inventive mind, a critical stand should be retained: the sculpture of four illusionistic cubes by Anssi Asunta at the main entrance reminds the visitor not to rely on his or her own eyes.

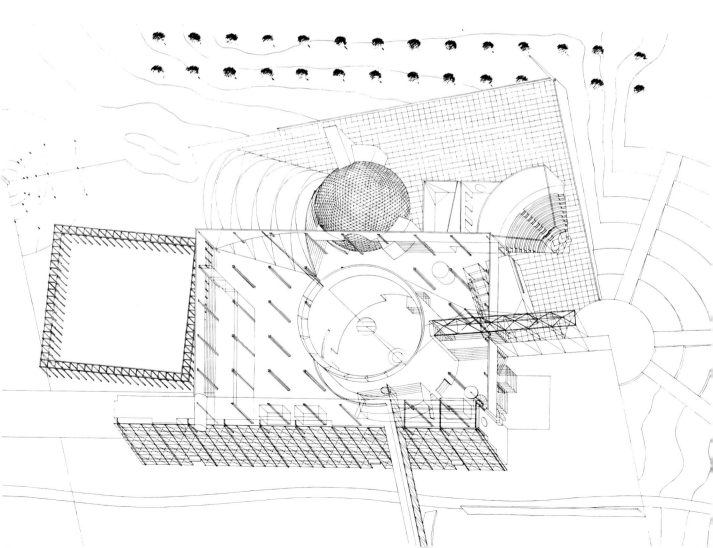

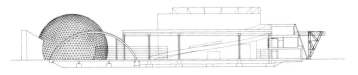

Section

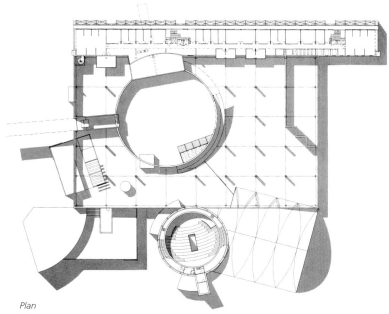

Plan

179

MIKKO HEIKKINEN

Born in Savonlinna, 1949

Work in various architectural offices, 1969–86

Master of Science in Architecture,
Helsinki University of Technology, 1975

Partner, Heikkinen - Komonen - Tiirikainen
Architects, 1974–78

Partner, Heikkinen - Komonen Architects, 1978–

State scholarship, 1989, 1995–97

Residence scholarship, New York,
Finnish Foundation of Visual Arts, 1992

Visiting teacher, Virginia Polytechnic, 1992

Residence scholarship, Paris, Cité des Arts, 1994

Visiting teacher, Städelschule Frankfurt, 1995

Instructor, Master Program Studio, Helsinki
University of Technology, 1997

MARKKU KOMONEN

Born in Lappeenranta, 1945

Work in various architectural offices, 1969–74

Master of Science in Architecture,
Helsinki University of Technology, 1974

Partner, Heikkinen - Komonen - Tiirikainen
Architects, 1974–78

Lecturer, Helsinki University of Technology, 1974–78

Editor in chief, *Arkkitehti* magazine, 1977–80

Partner, Heikkinen - Komonen Architects, 1978–

Director of Exhibition Department,
Museum of Finnish Architecture, 1978–86

State scholarship, 1982, 1988–90

Visiting teacher, Honors Studio,
University of Houston, 1983, 1993

Chairman of the board, Free Art School,
Helsinki, 1988–95

Visiting teacher, Virginia Polytechnic, 1992

Professor, Helsinki University of Technology, 1992–

HEIKKINEN - KOMONEN TEAM

The projects shown in this volume are due to the efforts of the following individuals:

Jussi Aulanko	1987–92	Kimmo Lintula	1996
Bill Bloomfield	1991	Iiro Mikkola	1990
Hanna Euro	1996–	Sarlotta Narjus	1989–
Simo Freese	1987–95	Janne Prokkola	1991
Kimmo Friman	1986–91	Markku Puumala	1996–
Harri Hakaste	1987	Mikko Rossi	1997–
Sampo Honkala	1988–92	Salla Rouhu	1990
Elina Huhtikangas	1986	Niklas Sandås	1990–
Riku Huopaniemi	1990–94	Niina Savolainen	1987–90
Leila Hyttinen	1986–88	Mona Schalin	1984–85
Maria Iivonen	1991–93	Antti-Matti Siikala	1992–93
Juha Ilonen	1987–89	Anu Sorsa	1993–
Juha Jääskeläinen	1995	Mikko Summanen	1995–
Janne Kentala	1984–	Merja Termonen	1989–91
Okke Kiviluoto	1990–96	Tuomas Toivonen	1997
Antti Könönen	1990–	Anna-Maija Tuunanen	1984
Sonja Liljeblad	1989–92		

PROJECT CHRONOLOGY

All dates, except as indicated, are completion dates.

Ecological Monitoring and Research Station,
Voj-Vozh, Russia, 1997–

Rovaniemi Airport Extension, Finland, 1997–
project architect: Mikko Rossi

Sauna for Finnish Ambassador's Residence,
Washington, D.C., 1997–

Cultural and Art Center Cable Factory Renovation,
· Helsinki, Finland, 1996–
project architect: Hanna Euro

Max Planck Institute for Molecular Biology and
Genetics, Dresden, Germany, 2000
project architect: Janne Kentala
associate architect: Henn Architekten Ingenieure,
Rudolf Röglin

Vuotalo Cultural Center, Helsinki, Finland, 2000
Competition, first prize
project architect: Niklas Sandås

Audiovisual Center for the University of Art and
Design, Helsinki, Finland, 1999
project architects: Sarlotta Narjus and Markku
Puumala

Vuosaari Gateway, Helsinki, Finland, 1999
project architect: Antti Könönen

Educational Unit for Poultry Farming, Kindia,
Guinea, 1998

Heureka Finnish Science Center Renovation, Vantaa,
Finland, 1998
project architect: Antti Könönen

Angel Studios, Helsinki, Finland, 1997
project architect: Antti Könönen

Elementary Schools, Madina Kouta and Boundou
Koura, Guinea, 1997

Herttoniemi Center Zoning Criteria, Helsinki,
Finland, 1997

Johns Hopkins University Student Art Center,
Baltimore, Maryland, 1997
Competition

McDonald's Headquarters, Helsinki, Finland, 1997
project architect: Janne Kentala

Museum of Contemporary Art—Stage Two
Development, Sydney, Australia, 1997
Competition

Cottage for Architecture Park, Copenhagen,
Denmark, 1996, and Stockholm, Sweden, 1998

Infocenter for Viikki Science Park, Helsinki, Finland,
1996
Competition

Teboil Rajahovi Service Station, Vaalimaa, Finland,
1996
project architect: Simo Freese

Arlanda Air-Traffic Control Center, Stockholm,
Sweden, 1995
Competition

Artcampus, Four Art Academies, Stockholm,
Sweden, 1995
Competition
project architect: Sarlotta Narjus

Helsinki Areena, Finland, project, 1995
project architect: Sarlotta Narjus

Helsinki Center Lighting Criteria, Helsinki, Finland,
1995
Competition

Media Center, Helsinki, Finland, 1995
Competition

Royal Theater—New Theater, Copenhagen,
Denmark, 1995
Competition

Senior Citizens' Home Renovation, Helsinki, Finland,
1995
project architect: Janne Kentala

Senior Officers' Training Unit, Emergency Services College, Kuopio, Finland, 1995
project architect: Janne Kentala

Villa Eila, Mali, Guinea, 1995

Arabianranta Design City, Hackmann Ltd. and University of Art and Design redevelopment study, Helsinki, Finland, 1994

Embassy of Nordic Countries, Berlin, Germany, project, 1994

Finnish Embassy, Washington, D.C., 1994
project architect: Sarlotta Narjus
associate architect: Angelos Demetriou & Assoc./ Eric Morrison

Foibe Senior Citizen Housing and Amenity Center, Vantaa, Finland, 1994
project architect: Janne Kentala

Health Center, Mali, Guinea, 1994

Workers' Institute Renovation, Helsinki, Finland, 1994

Modular Exhibition Pavilion for Marimekko, 1993–96
project architects: Simo Freese and Riku Huopaniemi

Centers for Karelian Culture, Kuhmo, Finland, and Kostamus, Russia, project, 1993

Children's Cabins, Housing Fair, Lahti, Finland, 1993

European Film College, Ebeltoft, Denmark, 1993
Competition, first prize, 1991
project architect: Sonja Liljeblad
associate architect: Nielsen, Nielsen & Nielsen/ Kim Herforth Nielsen

Free Art School Renovation, Helsinki, Finland, 1993

Museum of Contemporary Art, Helsinki, Finland, 1993
Competition

Onninen Ltd. New Visual Image, project, 1993
project architect: Simo Freese

Waterfront Concert Hall, Copenhagen, Denmark, 1993
Competition

Air Base for the Finnish Frontier Guard, Rovaniemi, Finland, 1992
project architect: Simo Freese

Airport Terminal, Rovaniemi, Finland, 1992
project architect: Simo Freese

Emergency Services College, Kuopio, Finland, 1992
Competition, first prize, 1988
project architects: Kimmo Friman and Sampo Honkala

Finnish and Swedish Embassies, Berlin, Germany, project, 1992

House of Culture, Nuuk, Greenland, 1992
Competition

Itäkeskus Shopping Center, Helsinki, Finland, 1992
project architect: Jussi Aulanko

Matrix H_2O Madrid, Spain, 1992
Exhibition

Gallén-Kallela Museum Renovation, Tarvaspää, Finland, 1991
with Juhani Pallasmaa

Halosenniemi Reception Building and Renovation, Pekka Halonen Atelier, Tuusula, Finland, 1991
with Juhani Pallasmaa

Lomapirtti Holiday Home, Pieksämäki, Finland, 1991
project architect: Janne Kentala

Munkinmäki Area, Kirkkonummi, Finland, 1991
Competition, second prize

Finnish Pavilion for a Nordic Art and Architecture Exhibition, Leeuwarden, The Netherlands, 1990

Maunula Cultural Center and Market, Helsinki, Finland, project, 1990

Finnish Pavilion for Expo in Seville, Spain, 1989
Competition

Hevosmiehentalo Renovation, Sinebrychoff Villa, Espoo, Finland, 1989
with Juhani Pallasmaa

Commercial Center Development Plan, Siilinjärvi, Finland, project, 1988

Heureka Finnish Science Center, Vantaa, Finland,
1988
Competition, first prize
project architect: Kimmo Friman

Bay Area Redevelopment, Lappeenranta, Finland,
1987
Competition

Center for Temporary Exhibitions, Helsinki, Finland,
1987
Competition

LomaNiemelä Vacation Hotel, Äänekoski, Finland,
1987
project architect: Janne Kentala

Sports and Leisure Area, Äänekoski, Finland, 1987
Competition, first prize

Artists' Village, Tuusula, Finland, project, 1986
with Juhani Pallasmaa

Saimaa Media Center, Lappeenranta, Finland,
project, 1986
with Juhani Pallasmaa

Lomakotien liitto ry Office Renovation, Helsinki,
Finland, 1985

Uutturanta Weekend Cottage, Jaala, Finland, 1985

Kotoranta Holiday Home Renovation, Kiljava,
Finland, 1984

Pyynikinlinna Manor House Renovation, Tampere,
Finland, 1984
project architect: Mona Schalin

Jyväskylä Library, Jyväskylä, Finland, 1975
Competition, third prize

Parish Center and Social Welfare Office,
Lappeenranta, Finland, 1973–77
with Jarmo Tiirikainen

Sports and Swimming Hall, Seinäjoki, Finland, 1972
Competition, second prize
with Tarkko Oksala and Jarmo Tiirikainen

SELECTED BIBLIOGRAPHY

Monographs

Heikkinen & Komonen (Barcelona: Gustavo Gili, 1994). Introduction by Peter Davey.

Korean Architects, June 1995. Introduction by Peter MacKeith.

Other Books

European Masters, Annual of Architecture, vol. 1 (Barcelona: Atrium, 1987).

Contemporary Architecture 90–91 (Lausanne: Presses Polytechniques et Universitaires Romandes, 1991).

European Masters, Annual of Architecture, vol. 3 (Barcelona: Atrium, 1991).

Maarten Kloos, ed., *Architecture Now* (Amsterdam: Architectura & Natura, 1991).

Kenneth Frampton, *Modern Architecture: A Critical History* (London: Thames & Hudson, 1992).

Scott Poole, *The New Finnish Architecture* (New York: Rizzoli, 1992).

Laura Pedrotti, "Centro Scientifico 'Heureka,'" in *Qualità Urbana in Europa* (Bologna: Fiere Internazionali di Bologna, 1993), 263–71.

Erik Nygaard, *Arkitektur i en forvirret tid* (Oslo: Christian Ejlers, 1994).

581 Architects in the World (Tokyo: TOTO Shuppen, 1995).

Josep M. Montaner, *Museums for the New Century* (Barcelona: Gustavo Gili, 1995).

Malcolm Quantrill, *Finnish Architecture and the Modernist Tradition* (London: E & FN, 1995).

Francisco Asensio Cerver, *Innovative Architecture* (Barcelona, 1996).

Bauen für die Sinne (Munich, 1996).

Contemporary European Architects, vol. 4 (Cologne: Taschen, 1996). Introduction by Philip Jodido.

William J. R. Curtis, *Modern Architecture since 1900* (London: Phaidon, 1996).

Jeremy Myerson, *New Public Architecture* (London: Laurence King, 1996).

Francisco Asensio Cerver, *The Architecture of Minimalism* (New York: Hearst Books International, 1997).

Christian W. Thomsen, *Sensuous Architecture* (New York: Prestel, 1998).

Exhibition Catalogs

Concrete in Finnish Architcture (Helsinki: Association of the Concrete Industries of Finland, Museum of Finnish Architecture, 1989).

An Architectural Present: 7 Approaches (Helsinki: Museum of Finnish Architecture, 1990).

Architektur, Kunsthandwerk, Malerei, Finnland 1900–1990 (Munich, 1990).

11 Cities, 11 Nations: Contemporary Nordic Art and Architecture (Leeuwarden, 1990).

Finskt I Nuet (Stockholm: Arkitektur Museet, 1990).

Quaternario 90, International Award for Innovative Technology in Architecture (Venice, 1990).

Workshop Prague '91 (Prague, 1991).

Contrasts & Connections (Helsinki: Expo '92 Finlandia, 1992).

Finland Builds, vol. 8 (Helsinki: Museum of Finnish Architecture, 1992).

Mies van der Rohe Pavilion Award for European Architecture (Barcelona, 1992).

Visiones para Madrid, Cinco ideas Arquitectonicas (Madrid, 1992).

Design for Architecture (Jyväskylä: Alvar Aalto Museum, 1995).

Kolonihaven: The International Challenge (Copenhagen: Rhodos International Science and Art Publishers, 1996).

Mies van der Rohe Pavilion Award for European Architecture (Barcelona, 1996).

New Finnish Architecture Photographed by Jussi Tiainen (Helsinki: Rakennuskirja, 1996).

Timber Construction in Finland (Helsinki: Museum of Finnish Architecture, 1996).

Finland Builds, vol. 9 (Jyväskylä: Museum of Finnish Architecture, 1998).

Symposium Publications

Architecture, Craftmanship and Design, International Conference on Architecture, Urban Planning and Design (Espoo, 1989).

The 5th International Alvar Aalto Symposium (Jyväskylä, 1992).

Articles

Arkkitehti, July 1986, 48–49. On the Uutturanta Weekend Cottage.

Sebastiano Brandolini, "Il centro finlandese della scienza," Casabella 535 (1987): 56–63.

Skala 11 (1987): 6. On the Heureka Finnish Science Center.

Kaarin Taipale, "Heureka, Architecture of Science," Form Function Finland, April 1987, 18–23.

Arkkitehti, July 1987, 32–37. On the LomaNiemelä Vacation Hotel.

Casabella 562 (1989): 29. On the Heureka Finnish Science Center.

John Welsh, "Finnish in Style," Building Design 944 (1989): 16–17.

Eeva Siltavuori, "Heureka, a Learning Experience," Form Function Finland, March 1989, 28–33.

Arkkitehti, April 1989, 44–57. On the Heureka Finnish Science Center.

Janey Bennet, "Recent Works of the Post-Aalto Generation," Architecture, September 1989, 58–61.

Deutsche Bauzeitung, September 1989, 30–33. On the Heureka Finnish Science Center.

Baumeister, October 1989, 44–45. On the Heureka Finnish Science Center.

Juliana Balint, "Eureka," L'Arca 36 (1990): 8–17.

Living Architecture 9 (1990): 94–103. On the Heureka Finnish Science Center.

Risto Pitkänen, "L'art de poser la bonne question," Formes Finlandaises 1990, 26–33.

Peter Davey, "Heureka Elements," Architectural Review, March 1990, 30–36.

Carel van Bruggen, "Fins Wetenschapsmuseum te Vantaa," de Architect, March 1990, 31–37.

Detail, April 1990, 389–94. On the Heureka Finnish Science Center.

Werk, Bauen + Wohnen, April 1990, 12–15. On the Heureka Finnish Science Center.

Arkkitehti, June 1990, 40–41, 56–59. On the Airport Terminal, Rovaniemi.

A+U, July 1990, 7–29. Roger Connah on the Heureka Finnish Science Center.

M. H. Contal, "Heureka," Architecture interieure créée, August–September 1990, 138–41.

John Welsh, "Claus and Effect," Building Design, December 1990.

Arkitekten 17 (1991): 510–23. On the competition for the European Film College.

Casabella 585 (1991): 36–38. On the Prague '91 workshop.

Design Journal 43 (1991): 16. Riitta Nikula on the Heureka Finnish Science Center.

Renato Morganti, "Il Centro Finlandese delle Scienza," L'industria delle costruzioni 233 (1991): 26–33.

Arkkitehti, January 1991, 82–84. On the Finnish Pavilion for a Nordic Art and Architecture Exhibition.

Hans de Moor, "Cultuurpaleizen in Finland," *Archis,* January 1991, 21–33.

Arkkitehti, April–May 1991, 35–38, 39–43. On the Finnish Embassy, Washington, D.C., and the European Film College.

Bauwelt, May 1991, 166–67. On the Heureka Finnish Science Center.

Juha Ilonen, "Architecture at the Intersection of Science and Art," *Casabella* 593 (1992): 4–17.

Annika Nyberg, "El Aeropuerto de Rovaniemi," *Form Function Finland*, special issue in Spanish, 1992, 82–85.

"Opere recenti di Heikkinen - Komonen," *Casabella* 593 (1992): 4–17.

Kaarin Taipale, "Two Roads to Nature," *Report* 2–3 (1992): 22–23.

Martha Thorne, "Visiones para Madrid: Cinco pro-puestas foráneas," *Arquitectura Viva* 27 (1992): 65.

John Welsh, "Jewel in a Paste Crown," *Building Design* 1095 (1992): 10.

Peter MacKeith, "Architecture + Art: Finnish Collaborations," *Form Function Finland,* January 1992, 60–65.

Baf nytt, February 1992, 6. On the Airport Terminal, Rovaniemi.

William Morgan, "A Century of Competitions in Finland," *Competitions,* February 1992, 42–49.

Arkkitehti, April–May 1992, 52–59. Maija Kairamo on the Airport Terminal, Rovaniemi.

Architectural Record, May 1992, 24. On the Finnish Embassy, Washington, D.C.

Scott Poole, "Foreign Brief: Finland," *Progressive Architecture,* May 1992, 154–55.

Arkkitehti, July–August 1992, 81–83. On Matrix H_2O Madrid.

Architektur + Wettbewerbe 156 (1993): 22–23. On the Emergency Services College.

Arquitectura Viva 30 (1993), special issue on Finnish architecture, 38–41, 42–45. On the Emergency Services College and the Airport Terminal, Rovaniemi.

Gudjón Bjarnason, "Finnsk hönnun á framabraut," *Arkitektur og skipulag*, 1993, 74–78.

Todd Dalland, "Structural Detailing," *L'Arca* 73 (1993).

Renato Morganti, "Due opere recenti," *L'industria delle costruzioni* 264 (1993): 26–37.

Arkkitehti, January 1993, 24–33. Juha Jääskeläinen on the Emergency Services College.

Clifford Pearson, "Following the Sun," *Architectural Record,* February 1993, 40.

Arkkitehti, March 1993, 44–45. On the Health Center, Mali.

Peter Davey, "Fine Finnish," *Architectural Review,* March 1993, 52–54.

Peter Davey, "Visual Acoustics," *Architectural Review,* April 1993, 81.

Leif Leer Sørensen, "Danske projekter," *Arkitekten,* May 1993, 198.

Lars Thiis Knudsen, "Bold and Brutal Boxes," *Arkkitehti,* June 1993, 72–81.

Magyar Épitömüvészet, June 1993, 18–21. On the Airport, Rovaniemi.

Jan W. Hänsen, "Minimalistiske kasser," *Arkitektur DK,* July 1993, 284–93.

Ehituskunst, August 1993, 37–41. On the House of Culture, Nuuk.

Peter MacKeith, "Emergency Finnish," *Architectural Review,* August 1993, 57–61.

Eva Janson, "Circle of Light," *Architectural Record,* September 1993, 67–71.

Bauwelt 40–41 (1994): 2288–91. On the Finnish Embassy, Washington, D.C.

Sebastiano Brandolini, "Ambasciata di Finlandia a Washington D.C.," *Casabella* 617 (1994): 54–59.

Domus 759 (1994): 20–25. On the European Film College.

Marie-Christine Loriers, "Chambres claires," *Techniques et Architecture* 414 (1994): 26–31.

William Morgan, "The Soul of Finland in the Heart of Washington," *Scandinavian Review*, 1994, 76–81.

Raymond Ryan, "Mikko Heikkinen & Markku Komonen: La nouvelle architecture finlandaise," *Neuf-Nieuw* 169 (1994): 10–16.

Arkkitehti, February–March 1994, 22–31. On the Finnish Embassy, Washington, D.C.

Claes Caldenby, "Teorin i praktiken, reflektionen kring kritikens gränser," *Nordisk arkitektur forskning,* March 1994, 65–74.

Katriina Jauhola-Seitsalo, "A Building that Blends In," *Form Function Finland,* March 1994, 4–9.

Henry Miles, "Freeze Frame," *Architectural Review,* June 1994, 78–83.

William Morgan, "The Cosmic Connection: The Architecture of Heikkinen and Komonen," *Progressive Architecture,* July 1994, 74–83.

Dietmar Danner, "Film ab," *AIT,* July–August 1994, 58–63.

Juliana Balint, "Für Elterns kein Zutritt," *MD,* September 1994, 63–64. On the Children's Cabins, Housing Fair, Lahti.

William Morgan, "Diplomatic Community," *Architectural Review,* October 1994, 36–42.

Clifford A. Pearson, "Diplomatic Maneuvers," *Architectural Record,* November 1994, 60–67.

Beatrice Houzelle, "Esprit nordique," *Techniques et Architecture* 422 (1995): 96–101.

Eva Janson, "Aeroporto de Rovaniemi," *Projeto* 185 (1995): 46–48.

Soledad Lorenzo, "Embajada de Finlandia en Washington: El paisaje en la memoria," *Diseño Interior* 44 (1995): 38–47.

William Morgan, "Die Seele Finnlands in Herzen Washingtons," *Architektur Aktuell* 184 (1995): 52–63.

Renato Morganti, "Heikkinen e Komonen, tre opere degli anni novanta," *L'industria delle costruzioni* 281 (1995): 20–39.

"The Power of Architecture," *Architectural Design,* 1995, 50–51.

"Scandinavians," *Arquitectura Viva* 55 (1995): 94–97.

Wif Stenger, "Embassy Takes the Washington Spotlight," *Design in Finland 1995,* 6–12.

"Architektur aus Finnland," *Der Architekt,* January 1995, 26–31.

Teppo Jokinen, "Schule für Rettungsdienste in Kuopio," *Baumeister,* January 1995, 30–35.

Juliana Balint, "Finnland Für 'Gläserne' Diplomatie," *Häuser,* February 1995, 10.

Arkkitehti, February–March 1995, 56–61. On the Foibe Senior Citizen Housing and Amenity Center.

Marcin Wlodarczyk, "Finlandia w Ameryce," *Arkitektura & Biznes,* March 1995, 12–13.

Detail, May 1995, 845–50. On the Finnish Embassy, Washington, D.C.

Roman Hollenstein, "Die grüne Botschaft," *NZZ Folio,* June 1995, 78–79.

Design Book Review 37–38 (1996): 53. On the Foibe Senior Citizen Housing and Amenity Center.

Domus 786 (1996): 10–17. On the Elementary Structures, Guinea.

Mikko Heikkinen, "Architecture Beyond Philosophical Ideas," *OZ* 18 (1996): 18–23.

"Scandinavian Architecture on the Top of the World," *Hinge* 27 (1996): 20–21.

Jan Verwijen, "A Big Dream," *Form Function Finland,* January 1996, 36–41.

Christoffer Harlang, "Beriget enkelhed," *Arkitekten,* February 1996, 42. Review of *Heikkinen & Komonen.*

Sabine Weissinger, "Finnische Botschaft Washington," *Glasforum,* February 1996, 3–6.

Simo Freese, "Fulanitalon työmaalla," *Arkkitehti,* February–March 1996, 32–35. On the Health Center, Mali.

Arkkitehti, April 1996, 42–45, 46–49. On the McDonald's Headquarters and the Teboil Rajahovi Service Station.

Michael Webb, "Arctic Stars: Finnish Design," *Metropolis,* April 1996, 62–65.

Arkkitehti, May–June 1996, 52–55. On the Vuosaari Gateway.

Ned Cramer, "Architects Update Danish Summer Houses," *Architecture,* October 1996, 44.

Arquis, November 1996, 42–47. On the Emergency Services College.

A+U 326 (1997): 40–47. On Villa Eila.

Armelle Lavalou, "Dispensaire et villa à Mali, Guinée," *L'architecture d'aujourd'hui* 309 (1997): 22–27.

"Light in Architecture," *Architectural Design,* 1997, 82–87.

Monument 18 (1997): 86–89. On the Finnish Embassy, Washington, D.C.

Ottagono 125 (1997): 46–48. On the Audiovisual Center for the University of Art and Design and Angel Studios.

Maria Stieglitz, "Kolonihaven: A Showcase for Eclecticism," *Scandinavian Review,* 1997, 59–64.

Space Design, October 1997, 43–45. On the Finnish Embassy, Washington, D.C.

Detail, January 1998, 56–60. On the Health Center, Mali.

Christoph Affentranger, "Finnische Architektur," *Bauwelt,* October 1998, 460–65.

PHOTOGRAPHY AND MODEL CREDITS

Unless noted below, all photographs and drawings have been provided by Heikkinen - Komonen Architects. Numbers refer to page numbers.

Photography
Fotark: 179
Eila Kivekäs: 82 top
Matti Pyykkö:14, 38, 40, 183 right
Simo Rista: 142, 145
Jussi Tiainen: 7, 8, 10, 22, 24, 26, 28, 30 top, 32–33, 35, 36, 37, 46, 48–49, 50, 51, 52, 53, 59, 60, 64, 65, 70, 71, 72, 74, 75, 76, 77, 78, 90, 91, 94, 95, 96, 97, 98, 100, 101, 102, 103, 104, 105, 106, 107, 108, 110–11, 112, 113, 114–15, 117, 118, 120–21, 122, 123, 124, 125, 128, 130, 131, 132, 133, 134, 136, 138 left, 140–41, 146, 147, 148, 150, 151, 153, 154–55, 157, 158, 159, 160, 162, 164–65, 166, 167, 172–73, 174, 176, 177, 178, 179, 180–81, 182, 183 left
Onerva Utriainen: 85, 86, 87
Sakari Viika/Comet: 168, 169, 170

Models
Olli-Pekka Keramaa: 8, 10
Ari Rahikainen: 7, 24, 46, 48, 50, 51, 52, 53, 70, 71
Risto Siitonen: 133
Klaus Stolt: 22, 60, 64, 65, 90, 91, 95, 97, 110, 118, 142, 145, 146, 147, 148 bottom, 150, 151, 153, 154–55, 157